:=:+:=:+:=:+:=:+:=:+:=:+

Willingness to heal is the prerequisite for all healing

:=:+:=:+:=:+:=:+:=:+:=:+:=:+:=:+:=:+:=:

Bruce Dickson, MSS, MA

Best Practices in Energy Medicine Series

Resources by and for kinesiology testers

For all therapeutic modalities ♥

Tools That Heal Press

HealingToolbox.org

The thing we are looking for,

is the thing we are looking with.
~ Ernest Holmes, Founder of Religious Science

The future is already here;
it's just not very well distributed yet
~ William Gibson, author, *Neuromancer*

"Willingness to heal
is the prerequisite for all healing"
Copyright " 2011 by Bruce Dickson
Published by Bruce Dickson on CreateSpace

ISBN-10: 0984162585

Other publisher inquiries welcome

To Learn More:
http://HealingToolbox.org
http://wholistic.theholisticchamberofcommerce.com
Bruce also recommends http://MSIA.org

The best solution is always loving
If you get stuck, give me a call.

v\V/v

Tools That Heal Press

Resources for the Hero's Journey of self-healing for self-healers and Energy Medicine practitioners

All books below available in PAPER with diagrams-charts; or, eBook without most images. All written with humor and insight by a practicing Health Intuitive.

Newest titles:

Muscle Testing for Success; Muscle-testing exercises applied to success topics. Simultaneously published as *Success Kinesiology, Dowsing for Success* and *Muscle Testing for Success*. All editions virtually the same except for unique covers.

Unconscious Patterns 101, Tools for the Hero's Journey of Self-healing
Picking up where NLP metaprograms left off, expanding the topic in the context of 'God is my Partner.'

Muscle Testing as Spiritual Exercise; Building a Bridge to Your Body's Wisdom. Muscle testing training redesigned with 'God as your Partner'

.v\V/v.

You are a Hologram Becoming Visible to Yourself - Making the invisible part of the "bigger you" visible and perceptible.

Your Habit Body, An Owner's Manual Our habits are our best friends; why then, do we make the same errors over and over again?

- **Self-Healing 101! Seven Experiments in Self-**

healing, You Can Do at Home to Awaken the Inner Healer, 2nd edition

- ***Meridian Metaphors,*** Psychology of the Meridians and Major Organs

- "***Willingness to heal*** is the pre-requisite for all healing" revised edition coming 2014

- ***You Have Three Selves Vol ONE***; Simply the clearest model of the whole person; Orientation

- ***You Have Three Selves; Vol TWO***, Find the 3S in your life & pop culture

- ***The Inner Court***: Close-up of the Habit Body

- ***The NEW Energy Anatomy***: Nine new views of human energy; No clairvoyance required.

- ***Radical Cell Wellness—Especially for women!*** Cell psychology for everyone; A coherent theory of illness and wellness

- ***The Five Puberties,*** Growing new eyes to see children afresh

- ***How We Heal; and, Why do we get sick?*** Including 35 better, more precise questions on wellness and healing, answered by a Medical Intuitive

- ***You have FIVE bodies PACME***; Spiritual Geography 101

- ***The Meaning of Illness is Now an Open Book,*** Cross-referencing illness and issues

Rudolf Steiner's Fifth Gospel in Story Form Topics include the TWO Jesus children and the active participation of the Buddha in the Christ event.

COMING *Measuring with 'God as your Partner;'*

HealingToolbox.org

Scales of 1-10, math and geometry
Cover images and longer descriptions at end of this book

Table of Contents

Chapter 1 ~ Unlearning — 12

How I learned about willingness from Bertrand — 12

Willingness vs. reactivity — 18

Infants have healthy willingness — 18

Tho invisible, willingness is highly conditioned — 18

Willingness and will — 19

Willingness and choice — 19

Willingness as the principle "To do better next time" ~ Rudolf Steiner — 20

Babies do not "surrender" — 20

A brief history of willingness — 22

Rollo May, *Love and Will* — 23

Being of two minds is what fractures willingness — 25

Two minds because two nervous systems — 25

Both selves need to work together as teammates — 28

When we are of TWO minds — 28

Example of being of two minds	29
Excess reactivity as cause of two minds	29
How to test if you are of two minds	29
Two beginner ways to self-muscle-test, you can do at home	30
Arm-length-testing, you can do at home	31
Difference between people who heal easily and people who heal slowly	31

Chapter 2 ~ You have five bodies, Spiritual Geography 101 — 33

Experience your five bodies RIGHT NOW	33
Two simple spiritual geographies	34
The map of Creation in your own hands	36
Stacking liquids, striated liquids	40

Chapter 3 ~ How does Spirit view my illness? — 45

Only two kinds of problems	46
Disease are lessons trickling down from ACME into our physical body	48
Redeeming the imagination	50

Willingness to change my comfort zone   51

Chapter 4 ~ Reactivity interrupts willingness 51

Excess Liking & Disliking   52

Reactivity cancels healthy focus   53

Reactivity: "I knew it was bad for me and I did it anyway"
                                                      54

Healthy & unhealthy willingness   55

Chapter 5 ~ Dysfunctions of Willingness   56

The child is mother to the woman   59

Stephen Colbert's parody of willfulness, wontfulness, resistance & againstness   59

Willfulness blocks willingness to heal   60

Chapter 6 ~ Where is willingness located in my body?
                                                      62

'Inner Court' innovation   65

Chapter 7 ~ Measuring willingness to heal   67

Two measures, one from neck-up, another from neck-down
65

Chapter 8 ~ Check willingness to heal FIRST in your sessions   71

How I used to do sessions   72

Case study: How I do sessions now   74

Chapter 9 ~ Where's my magic pill? I want to be healed NOW!   79

Managing your expectations   79

Chapter 10 ~ Other things you can measure   81

Your Ring of Success is made up of six links   83

Four categories of human issues in Book of Genesis   85

Issues with God and your own Divinity   86

Possible additional major categories   87

Chapter 11 ~ Willingness in groups and group process   87

Willingness and the consensus process	87
So what replaces Robert Rules of Order?	90
Quieting the "safety brain"	92
"Collaborative awareness" vs. "self awareness"	93
FIVE Components of Blueprint of WE	93
Willingness and living NOW	94
The Plan for human beings	95
Willingness and children	95

About the Author 96

Tools That Heal Press Booklist	97
Best Practices in Holistic Self-Healing Series	97
The two best sellers	97
Works incidental & complementary to Best Practices Series, above	128
Connect with the Author	132
Sessions with the author	132
Training with the Author	133
Other products	134
Reading Group Guide for Self-healing Series	134
Books outside the Best Practices Series	136
Stand-alone 99 cent eBooks tangential to Best Practices Series	136
Other CLASSICS of self-healing & Medical Intuition	136

Chapter 1:

Unlearning

> It's not what people know already that's the problem; the problem is, what people know that *t'ain't so*--that's the problem ~ Josh Billings, 1930s news commentator

Willingness to heal is the pre-requisite for all healing -- Bertrand Babinet (Babinetics.com)

A corollary: Willingness to change is the prerequisite to all change.

The truth of Bertrand's words hardly needs commentary. Self-healing takes place optimally and speedily where and when willingness to heal is present.

The whole topic of "will" is far too large to tackle here. We only address purposes of self-healing here.

How I learned about willingness from Bertrand

Well it's invisible. You can't touch, see, or taste willingness; you cannot carry it in a wheelbarrow. Yet like loving, vitality and intimacy, healthy willingness is an invisible quality we all desire and yearn towards.

I met Bertrand Babinet around 1985, an acupuncturist and energetic healer, thru Movement of Spiritual Inner Awareness in Los Angeles. He innovated a large number of topics. Way beyond acupuncture, Touch for Health or NLP, he opened up access to the sub- and unconscious beyond anything anyone had done up until then by a couple orders of magnitude.

Interested students of his, able to self-muscle-test, were able to follow his ideas, absorb them, work them, and innovate further upon them.

Unfortunately no organization grew up around Bertrand to preserve his innovations. They were taken up into PTS MSS-DSS in a highly transformed way. Healing Toolbox has attempted to preserve Bertrand's original ideas--in more accessible form--and document innovations developed from them made since.

It was momentous. For the first time ever, using self-muscle-testing, myself and his other students could learn what was happening in our own sub- and unconscious with clarity way beyond Gestalt, Transactional Analysis, Touch for health, or NLP had provided us.

Not only could did Bertrand provide navigational tools, he innovated many new clearing techniques and methods.

Because Babinetics was strongly body-based, it remained grounded. The words did matter as much as finding in your own body and psyche what his words pointed to.

This empowered his students to explore and persist in their attempts to clear persistent core disturbances that had not yielded to other modalities.

Babinetics was NOT the only set of "power tools" for muscle testers developed around the Alternative

Decade of the Brain, 1990-2000. It was, however, a noticeably more-effective set of power tools compared with other Energy Medicine methods before or since.

Q: Why was Babinetics more effective than other Energy Medicine methods-techniques?

A: I think of several reasons:

1) Babinetics connects itself, and users, with a positive, healthy, ecumenical spirituality, as expressed in MSIA.org. Coupling any Energy Medicine method-technique with a loving, ecumenical spirituality, increases its simplicity and elegance because Oneness stands behind it and informs the method via the archetypes accessed.

2) Babinetics has strong, effective psychic self-protection routines built into it, many of them taken from MSIA.org.

Coupling any Energy Medicine method-technique with a loving, ecumenical spirituality, increases spiritual protection from above your mind. The more powerful a tool is, the more needed are safety and protection measures. The most powerful Energy Medicine techniques call for the most powerful psychic-spiritual self-protection. Make sense?

Above merely mental-logical human thinking, is the holistic thinking of the Angels. You want Angels of upward spirals on your side in your self-healing. You get them on your side by asking for their Guidance and connecting your Energy Medicine method-technique with a loving, ecumenical spirituality, of your own choosing.

Can you think of a way to say this more simply? If you can, share with me.

3) Babinetics is consciously based on the Three Selves model of our psyche, the simplest clearest model of the whole-person. Oneness also stands behind the model of the Three Selves, informing it,

4) In retrospect, it's now clearer how Babinetics dovetails more closely with Goethean Holistic Science than some Energy Medicine methods. Reframing the Steiner-Anthroposophic topic of "Goethean science" into 'Goethean Holistic Science,' seems to expose the biggest, natural, underlying support for holistic health and healing in all forms and expressions. This conversation has begun at http://blog.goetheanscience.net   You are welcome to engage.

Goethean Holistic Science is a natural support foundation because it encourages individuals to:

- Choose a topic they wish to explore and a method they wish to employ,

- Perform simple, little home experiments for TWO ends,

- To learn about the Nature of their subject of investigation; and,

- To increase their self-sensitivity towards their subject; in a phrase, self-development.

Babinetics uses this method, encourages this sequence. This is its connection with Goethean science.

ANY Energy Medicine method using this simple framework connects with Goethean science. We just forgot Goethe's and Steiner's approach in a couple centuries of corporate-consumer-driven-science.

Let's contrast Babinetics with meridian tapping (TFT-EFT-TAT).

In the latter, you follow a tapping "recipe" which in a great many cases will work and is safe. Meridian-tapping experiments are some of the simplest Goethean Holistic Science experiments imaginable. That's why they are so effective; that's why meridian tapping is so popular. That's ONE Tool That Heals.

In all the more professional-grade Energy Medicine systems, experimenters are given a much larger Healing Toolbox of Tools That Heal.

Q: Examples of "professional-grade" Energy Medicine methods?

A: Chiropractic, osteopathy, BodyTalk, Peace Theological Seminary Doctorate Program, Oriental Medicine herbs+acupuncture, Touch for Health, Theta Healing, possibly Donna Eden's Meridian Tracing training, maybe a few others.

Each of these is akin to a child's chemistry lab kit, a set of generally-regarded-as-safe methods-techniques you apply in simple home experiments, as convenient and comfortable for you.

Around 1990 muscle testing and NLP were converged

in a framework of ecumenical spirituality. Babinetics was a the forefront here. Spiritual Response Therapy (SRT) was not far behind.

Once this convergence occurred, a reliable experimental method for addressing and navigating to invisible, unresolved, sub- and unconscious issues existed for the first time. This was new.

For the first time self-healers and holistic practitioners had adequate and sufficient tools to navigate invisible parts of the psyche until sooner or later, solutions were revealed. The new tools opened up many new avenues to pursue and follow therapeutic direction.

While Energy Medicine methods are frequently and unethically commercialized as panaceas and cure-alls, what's more true is Energy Medicine methods primarily work in the domain of only one person. Among other things, this is keeping us humble in a healthy way. Find full discussion of this in *Muscle Testing as a Spiritual Exercise*.

So for the most part, new Energy Medicine tools opened up many new avenues to pursue and follow therapeutic direction *in the domain of single individuals*.

Bertrand's contribution was acknowledged by John-Roger in many ways; including, a live, public talk-seminar by J-R on Bertrand's methods. The copyright to this seminar was given outright to Bertrand for his use. Only EyeClasses was similarly gifted by John-Roger, before or since, to my knowledge.

Bertrand produced a book, *Healing the Inner Family*,

now out of print. He says he wants to make it available as an eBook. I hope he does, soon. The absence of documentation for Babinetics was a large motivator for Tools That Heal Press.

Willingness vs. reactivity

Babinetics innovated the polarity of willingness vs. reactivity. You can picture these as two kids on a see-saw, a teeter-totter, when one is up, the other is down; hence, the cover of this book. The other cover prepared pictured a caterpillar becoming a butterfly, an image of 'willingness to change.'

Bertrand demonstrated over and over in his work with individuals how reducing reactiveness, you increase willingness. Willingness is the healthy state; reactiveness is a disturbed state. The more we can clear reactivity in the sub- and unconscious levels of our psyche, the more our own natural knowing of Oneness can resume.

What do infants have? They have healthy willingness

When we are born, what do we exhibit in our behavior?

What is happy new baby behavior primarily? It is not "will;" it is not "willfulness." We certainly do not have "will power."

As healthy babies, what we have is willingness.

This is what we are trying to get back to as adults on any path of personal-spiritual growing: healthy willingness.

Tho invisible, willingness is highly conditioned

Rudolf Steiner suggests most of which makes us truly human is invisible. What makes us most truly human remains primarily invisible.

This is good to keep in mind to counter all the propaganda of "what you see is what you get." Not so in our psyche; rather, what you *don't see* is what you primarily get; 90% of what you get is what you don't see. Just ask anyone who got married or who had a child recently.

As part of Creation, invisible things are still highly conditioned and patterned. In psychology, NLP and MBTI demonstrate how the human habit body, which is mostly unconscious, is highly patterned and conditioned, the home of many patterns. In TA they call these "games. In NLP they call them "metaprograms." In Healing Toolbox, we call them Unconscious Patterns.

Our unconscious—thought to be inaccessible until the Alternative Decade of the Brain, 1990-2000, exhibits many patterns easy to grasp, become familiar with and use as navigational reference points. Willingness is one of these Unconscious patterns stable enuf to be a reference point when exploring.

Willingness and will

Willingness is a use of will, as in "willing to go along;" and, "willing to be flexible."

Willingness and choice

Soul is choice. We have choice in whether to go along

with the way things are going; or, resist and assert our voice for a new course and direction.

Willingness as the principle "To do better next time" ~ Rudolf Steiner

Rudolf Steiner, a fully clairvoyant educator, founder of Waldorf-method education, who died 1925, came closest to Bertrand's modern definition of willingness.

Babies do not "surrender"

Babies do not "surrender," in any adult sense. Rudolf Steiner, the founder of Waldorf education characterized babies as psychic "sponges" willingly soaking up impressions, percepts of every available kind, in order to begin comprehending its new environment. With nothing to compare this world to, as infants we have high willingness towards our world and our family.

For adult minds: Willingness is the choice to yield the rigid boundaries of the isolated single self in order to align with something larger than, or outside, the isolated single self.

We are much better off beginning by listening to Rudolf Steiner, NLP, William Glasser and NVC (Compassionate Communication, CNVC.org) and characterizing the activity of willingness. This is how to get at it. Willingness is not a thing you can put in a wheelbarrow and carry, as NLP observes. It's alive and so, has character.

Yes, Willingness is invisible. You can't touch, see, feel or taste willingness. Like loving, life and intimacy, willingness is an invisible we all grapple with and perhaps yearn towards.

Willingness is, and is not, "surrender"

Willingness can be "healthy surrender;" as in "surrender to a higher power;" and, "subordinating your agenda" to a higher good.' Willingness can mean subordinating the agenda of your isolated single self, to the needs of your spouse, your children, community, the large whole.

A common expression of healthy willingness is service to self and service to others. "Service is the highest form of consciousness on the planet" (John- Roger). It's a sign of maturity to choose the greatest good for the greatest number, in ever widening circles, around us.

Unhealthy surrender can be acquiescing, giving up or not caring; as in, "whatever," or "anything goes."

We always want to preserve choice, to keep our self choosing more of what we want, less of what we do not want.

The connotations of "surrender" have evolved more than most words in English since "surrender" in the 1800s meant either:

- A defeated people surrendering to a Napoleon; laying down arms. In old-school paternalism, "surrender" was only for sissies; domination was the preferred masculine value; or

- A romantic, hysterical individual woman swooning into passivity, a feminine expression seen in movies as late as the 1930s and at Frank Sinatra concerts in the 1940s; or

I suspect in 2014 both healthy "surrender" and healthy "willingness" have to be redeemed and purified from the negative connotations of "necessarily wimpy."

Enriching matters, healthy surrender and healthy willingness have to be correlated with functional King Arthur. At his most magnificent, Arthur represents healthy moral fiber, moral character and appropriate use of physical strength and force.

If the concept "willingness" is still unclear to you, you are not alone. The meanings of "will," "willpower" and therefore "willingness" have been changing, more or less continually since they were, perhaps, the first popular topic of "scientific psychology," in the early and middle 1800s. Rollo May, below, has a great summary of this culturally evolving meaning of "will." Let's get to a practical definition.

A brief history of willingness

The early history of psychology in the 1800s and this history viewed thru Rudolf Steiner, tells how "Will" and "willpower" were THE hotly contested terms in academia, even before there was any discipline calling itself "psychology." Coming to terms with and defining "Will" and "willpower" was a favorite topic at dinner parties just as The Law of Attraction and quantum physics were in the 1990s.

Looking back from the post-2012 world, we can see the conversation got off to many false starts. Compared to their contemporaries, Freud, Jung, Steiner, Adler and Reich did indeed have better ideas about "will" and "will power.

The problem was everyone from Kant to Reich meant

something different by "will." They had the classic "Blind Men and the Elephant" situation, each holding one part of the creature, thinking their one part characterized the totality of the creature.

Steiner's ideas on "will" are closest to a holistic view compatible with our thinking since 1970. I believe he wished "will" to equate with what we now call the lower etheric formative forces, those forces that keep living physical matter together and operational. As we do today, Steiner excluded "soul" from "etheric forces."

Steiner's generation and the next two generations lacked reliable experimental methods to explore, verify and validate his concepts. These did not appear until about 1990.

A more clear picture of willingness emerged once the holistic health-healing era began in 1970 because the inner child was acknowledged. It became safe to talk about the inner child and not be laughed at. Still Muscle testing and NLP had to converge within a spiritual framework.

What Healing Toolbox adds to self-healing is first a Waldorf-methods approach to curricula development and topic sequencing. Second, Healing Toolbox adds a more stable theoretical foundation for Energy Medicine by transposing Steiner-Waldorf-Goethean science topics into holistic health and healing topics.

Rollo May, *Love and Will*

Rollo May's *Love and Will* (1969) contains a great summary of the evolving, very limited history of "what is will?" A sequence of excerpts:

Willpower was conceived by our 19th century forefathers as the faculty by which they made resolutions [to] direct their lives down the rational and moral road [conventional] culture said they should go (p 182).

One of Freud's great contributions... [was] under his penetrating analysis, Victorian 'will' indeed turned out to be [merely] a web of rationalizations and self-deceit. Freud's [new] image ...was of human beings no longer ...driving their own life; but rather, driven thru life by their unconscious urges, anxieties, fears and an endless host of bodily drives and instinctual forces.

In formulating a new image of humanity, Freud shook to the foundations Western man's emotional, moral and intellectual self-image [built up in the 1700s and 1800s] (p 183).

[The idea of] Willpower [in the 1800s] expressed the arrogant efforts of Victorian man to manipulate his surroundings and to rule Nature [women, children and many foreigners] with an iron hand. As well, to manipulate himself, rule his own [inner] life, in the same way he would an object (183).

[In 19th century thinking] This kind of [dysfunctional macho] 'will' was set over against [the more yin] 'wish.'

'Will' was used to suppress and deny 'wish' (183).

HealingToolbox.org

Victorian man sought, as Ernest Schachtel has put it, to deny that he had ever been a child, to repress his irrational tendencies and so-called infantile wishes--as all unacceptable to [conventional images] of being grown-up and responsible (p 205).

Willpower was a way of avoiding awareness of bodily and sexual urges... which did not fit the picture of the controlled, well-managed self (205).

Freud [identified this] 'will' as an implement in the service of repression, no longer a positive moving [and spiritualizing] force (p 207).

Consequently the word "will," which some people still define as a positive thing, in more modern terms, more commonly connotes a negative, referring backwards to all the familiar cultures of macho patriarchal domination.

Being of two minds is what fractures willingness

If you wish to heal--and nothing happens or you encounter resistance, then you are of two minds.

Lack of progress on your stated goals is the clearest evidence of being of two minds. See if any of these fit for you:

- I take two steps forward and then I seem to take one step back. Why is that?

- When I ask for what I want, people often walk away; or, I rarely ask for what I want.

- I'm never satisfied with myself no matter how much I do.

- I don't know what I want.

If any of these apply to you, join the club! We each have lots of these dysfunctions to work on. You are not alone!

Two minds because two nervous systems

We can be of two minds because we have two nervous systems. This is all by design, not a defect.

You have a cerebral nervous system, your brain, spine and spinal nerves, in the top and back of your physical body.

You have an enteric nervous system, less well-known, in your omentum, and in nervous tissue diffused thru the internal organs of digestion, assimilation and reproduction. This system is primarily in the front side of the solar plexus, below your diaphragm muscle.

One mind is your rational mind. One is your gut brain, your immune-system-self.

BOTH are intelligent but only one is dominant.

Ideally gut brain dominates between gestation and age 12. During this time you gather healthy self-esteem.

After puberty, ideally cerebral brain dominates. As an adult you gather healthy self-concept.

In adults, one mind is dominant and one mind is sub-dominant, just like right and left handedness. Either brain can be dominant. Individual variation is very common and crucially significant.

Your rational mind, either top or bottom, either prefers to make decisions thru thinking OR feeling. For a full discussion, see *You Have Three Selves, vol. 1*.

Q: You mean my gut brain can be dominant?

A: Absolutely. Our language does not accommodate this easily. English is strongly skewed towards the assumption your intellect, CNS, top brain, dominates. So we have to write that way, assume cerebral dominance as the default. Yet your other mind, your gut brain, your inner child, Little Artist, subconscious, habit body, operating system of the psyche--whatever you like to term it—can indeed be "running the show" in individuals.

This is less common in the industrialized and educated Western countries.

Being of two minds blocks willingness to heal 'Inner cooperation' means being of one mind, not two.

John-Roger says inner cooperation is the biggest karma on the planet. In Birth Plan numerology, the number two (2) symbolizes inner cooperation. Inner cooperation is the conscious self--the yak yak mind-- and basic self both being on the same page, both looking the same direction and seeing the same goal.

HealingToolbox.org

Both selves need to work together as teammates

In order to heal a body concern, your rational mind and your non-dominant mind both need to work as a team.

They need to be attending to the same concern and seeing the same healthy outcome. The more sensory detail VAKOG you can put on to your ideal scene of healing, the more reference points the inner child has to get you what you ask for; you are lined up inside. If your two minds are working together, cooperating, collaborating as a team, then healing happens easily.

The most dramatic examples of dysfunction, being of two minds, include, regretful unfaithful husbands, regretful binge eaters, secret cross-dressers, and thieves who feel guilty later.

Being of one mind on a goal is both minds united on the same goal.

When we are of TWO minds

When we are of two minds, our two selves are NOT working together as teammates.

Being of single mind, one focus on one dream, one goal, one passion increases our energetic strength. Your rational mind and non-dominant mind are both looking the same direction and seeing the same goal (J-R). They are working together, cooperating, collaborating teamed up. You have two minds and this is a good thing; like, having two hands.

Example of being of two minds

You, the conscious self, wish to heal issue X. The basic self has its eye elsewhere. Your basic self is aligned elsewhere. Your conscious self says, "Yes, I want to heal X." The basic self, the inner child, says, "No, not until I get what I want."

This means you are of two minds.

In more technical language, being of two minds occurs when the cerebral nervous system has one goal or intention and the enteric (gut) brain has another goal, intention or desire, another point of view.

If the rational mind is looking one way--your basic self may have its eye elsewhere. This sometimes manifests physically in the phenomena called "lazy eye."

Excess reactivity as cause of two minds

What causes us to be of two minds?

Being of two minds is usually caused by unmonitored excess reactivity. Bertrand Babinet suggests excess reactivity is what primarily causes us to split our inner forces and become "of two minds." He suggests excess reactivity is the main stumbling block in personal-spiritual growth.

How to test if you are of two minds

Q: How can I learn if I am of two minds?

The simplest way to test if you are of two minds is to make TWO tests, one form the neck up, a second test from the neck down.

Ultimately, "you don't have to know; you only have to ask" (Maryann Castellanos). You may not know you are of two minds, until you test.

Find more discussion of the neck-up neck-down polarity in articles at HealingToolbox.org.

Two beginner ways to self-muscle-test, you can do at home

Q: Well, I can't do muscle testing of any kind so I'm a lost cause.

A: Did you know Peace Theological Seminary introduced a new social way to do self-muscle-testing? I call it Client-Controlled Testing.

This compassionate innovation permits and encourages anyone, anywhere, whether they can self-muscle-test or not, to test as long as they have a neutral partner.

Q: Even me?

A: Yes, especially you. Using Client-Controlled-Testing (CCT) anyone wishing to do so, can test themselves.

How to test yourself using two people: Client Controlled Testing Client-Controlled Testing requires no skill at all. In fact, the less skill employed the better.

It does require two persons, one them a completely neutral and silent partner; the other, the tester-testee.

The tester-testee sets up the question—the partner observes. The tester-testee interprets results and determines the meaning of all results gained—the partner says nothing and observes.

The neutral partner is only the arm-pusher-downer AND NOTHING MORE. Using this method, absolutely anyone wishing to try K-testing CAN do so.

With tools this simple, anyone can pick a concern they wish to heal and measure their own willingness to heal.

You CAN do this. The time is right for this in the world now.

Arm-length-testing, you can do at home

As of 2013, the simplest solo self-muscle-testing is arm-length-testing. Dr. Uwe Albrecht of Germany promotes this at InnerWise.eu which has an English version. http://innerwise.com/en/videos/all-videos/113-innerwise-the-arm-lenght-test?category_id=54

Difference between people who heal easily and people who heal slowly

All the people who accomplish and complete healing in their body--or anywhere else--have high willingness to heal in common.

Conversely, people who never seem to heal, or who have relapses--have some things in common too.

The easy-healing people are of one mind on the issue they wish to heal. They are Coherent, Integrated and Aligned (CIA) on what they wish to change.

The slower-healing people are of two minds on their healing "target;" they lack high CIA.

This means most of us are unlearning willfulness, wontfulness, resistance and againstness. The vast majority of our willfulness, wontfulness, resistance and againstness is unconscious, in Delta. This means we only learn about these blocks as they arise in our awareness, which is naturally a long gradual process. This appears to be by design.

For a healing to take place, USUALLY the conscious and basic self have to BOTH be aligned toward the same goal.

I say "usually" because Grace is always a possibility. If Grace shows up, great; otherwise keep asking & looking for new directions on any issue you are stuck on.

For much inner movement to take place in a healing session, usually a person has to be of one mind, the basic self (b/s) has to be "on board," aligned with the same target your conscious self has selected.

The conscious and basic selves do not need to be 100% in alignment. This is rare so don't expect it. I find the b/s has to be at a 6/10 willingness to heal or higher, on the target issue, for me to feel confident movement can take place on that issue. The more in concert conscious and basic self are on healing the target, the better. Make sense?

If the basic self is NOT in concert 60% on healing the target, then you are still at listening to feelings and needs and negotiating what an agreed-upon target could be. What will be win-win for both your inner child and rational mind? Find something you and your basic self both wish to heal.

HealingToolbox.org

If all else fails, unconditional loving opens the book of the basic self.

Chapter 2:

You have five bodies; Spiritual Geography 101

Q: What's the goal of healthy willingness?

A: To have healthy willingness on each frequency of our psyche, PACMES.

20th century psychology gave us no simple, elegant want to conceive of our five bodies, our five levels of habits, our five levels of creativity, down here in the personality.

Fortunately the Light & Sound groups, Sound Current groups, have had a simple, elegant Spiritual Geography for 150 years at least, that makes it easy to grasp all this.

Spiritual Geography is worth hearing about because it aids in setting directions, directionality.

Did you ever find yourself lost in a giant shopping mall and in need of a bathroom? Did you ever breathe a sigh of relief when you finally found a mall map and diagram of the mall showing you where you are right now, and where your destination is, relative to where you are now? This is "directionality," the value of maps generally.

If you are confused about spiritual things, Spiritual Geography can lead to a similar sigh of relief because it shows the "lay of the land" you are walking. It's the lay of the land of our habit body, very useful if you ever wish to change or upgrade a habit.

Experience your five bodies RIGHT NOW

The best intro to spiritual geography is experiential. In the early 1970s a certain experiential meditation was popular and used in many learning settings to make clearer the five distinctions in our psyche. It goes like this:

Close your eyes. Quiet your pictures of what you like and dislike. Now quiet your feelings about what you love and hate. Now quiet your mind. Now quiet your memories.

Okay now--who's doing that?

The One doing the quieting–however well or poorly–is your soul, the spark of the immortal-eternal in you, in all of us.

Two simple spiritual geographies

Two simpler spiritual geographies will support us in grasping the scope of PACME.

The most simple versions of PACME, the simplest spiritual geography is:

Father-God ~ Mother-God.

Two regions or fields. Some of you will understand this is analogous to a magnet with north and south poles; Father-God as the North; Mother-God as the South.

Prefer an art analogy? The two are analogous to the love affair between Painter and Painting.

The Father Principle is the unchanging creaTING part.

The Mother Principle is the changing, flowing creatED part, the SUSTAINER of ONGOING Creation, the Horn of Plenty, the Cornucopia.

So Mother~Father leads to CreaTION and creaTING.

Their Son, the Holy Spirit, I think is easiest to imagine as the love, joy and synergy between Mother and Father God, the result of their creating. So the Earth, you, me and all of creation, is their Child, their Son, part of their creation. We came out of their joy of Mother~Father creating together.

So the simplest spiritual geography can also be represented in a diagram, one pole above, one pole below:

>   Unchanging, eternal, coherent, aligned, stable
>   but no fixed form.
>   **All the positive Qualities of consciousness**
>   -
>   Changing. Flowing. Temporary.
>   All conditioned energies and forms,
>   **all fixed forms consciousness can inhabit**

These two polarities face each other, as lovers do. More accurately, they are really interpenetrating. 3D creation, and all other levels of conditioned reality, are their offspring. If they ever stopped interpenetrating, the atoms would stop spinning and we'd all be in trouble.

In the human experience, in our body, mind, emotions, for all manifesting within form, we live, move and have our being within the Mother God.

In a physical body, we measure our material health, wealth and happiness primarily from our neck down.

In a physical body, as adults, we measure our freedom outside primarily from our neck up.

So that's the simplest map. Notice it embraces polarity as a healthy thing, just as it takes two poles of a car battery for a car to run.

The PACME model expands on this continuum idea distinguishing five frequencies within Creation. Taken together, these five reflect, in microcosm, the macrocosm of just Creation, the created part of God's body.

The map of Creation in your own hands

The simplest map of PACME+Soul is "at hand" in your two hands. Can you do this with your hands?

PACME+Soul

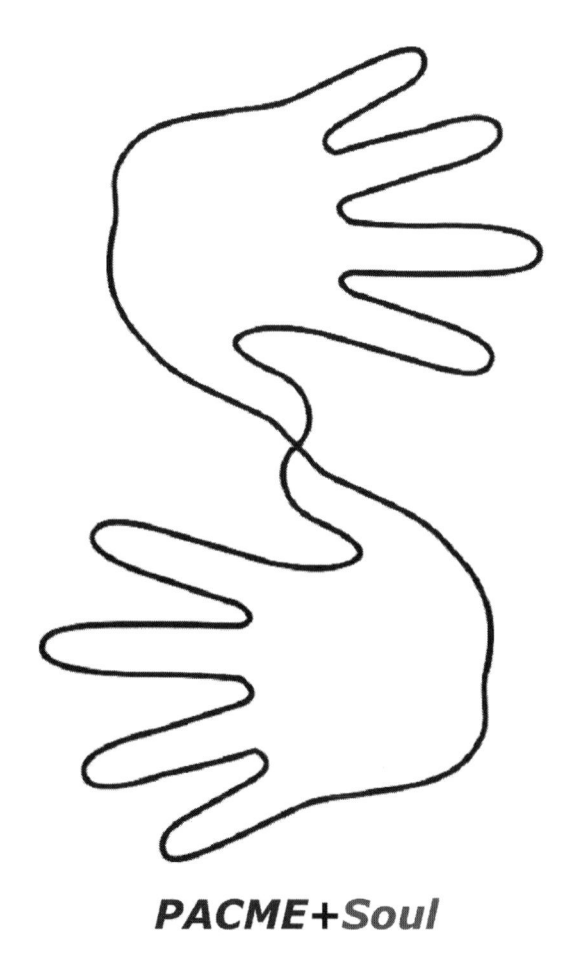

Dg-hands-model

Notice one hand is palm-out the other hand is palm-in. This suggests the additional not-so-obvious mirror effects the model has.

Your two hands should be in the same vertical plane as much as possible; for instance, NOT 90 degrees to each other. That's something else.

Your lower hand represents Creation. Your little finger pointing down on this hand, represents the physical level. The weakest finger naturally stands for the weakest of our five bodies, in terms of energy potential.

Your lower hand ring finger represents the level of liking, disliking, polarity and ambition (astral).

Your lower hand middle finger represents your deeper emotions. You have two strongest fingers on each hand, middle and thumb. Middle finger represents one of the two strongest of your five invisible bodies, in terms of energy potential, at this time in Creation. The original Theosophy name was the causal (emotional) realm. This is where the letter "C" comes from in PACME. Our causal-emotional body is the strongest level at this time in Creation.

Your lower hand pointer finger represents your mind-beliefs-judgments-evaluations. The finger we point with represents our mental activity—how convenient!

Your lower hand thumb is our other strongest finger. It points up. It represents our unconscious memories, habits, behaviors, role-models, archetypes, and fairy tales we live by. This is other strongest part of our psyche in Creation, our Habit Body, our comfort zones. This is the "flywheel" of our psyche so we don't have to re-learn how to walk all over again each day anew. It is the strength of stability, continuity, predictability.

Your top hand represents Soul and Above. The suggestion is these two face each other as equals, a picture of the wholeness and Oneness of God, of Mother~Father God.

The five fingers of your upper hand are not meant to

suggest the same stratification of frequencies and conditioning as exist below. The five fingers of our upper hand are pretty good place holders suggesting something is up there worth knowing about.

As souls here in the human experience, our five conditioned levels-bodies, physical, imaginative, emotional, mental and unconscious, are what we are charged with managing. Our job is to make healthy choices, as best we can, to do the right thing, at the right time, with the right people, for the right purpose--as Plato or Socrates said.

Stacking liquids, striated liquids

dg-striated liquids

Different frequencies naturally arrange themselves in an orderly fashion, slower, heavier ones below, faster-lighter ones on top.

LAMP OIL
RUBBING ALCOHOL
VEGETABLE OIL
WATER
DISH SOAP
MILK
100% MAPLE SYRUP
CORN SYRUP
HONEY

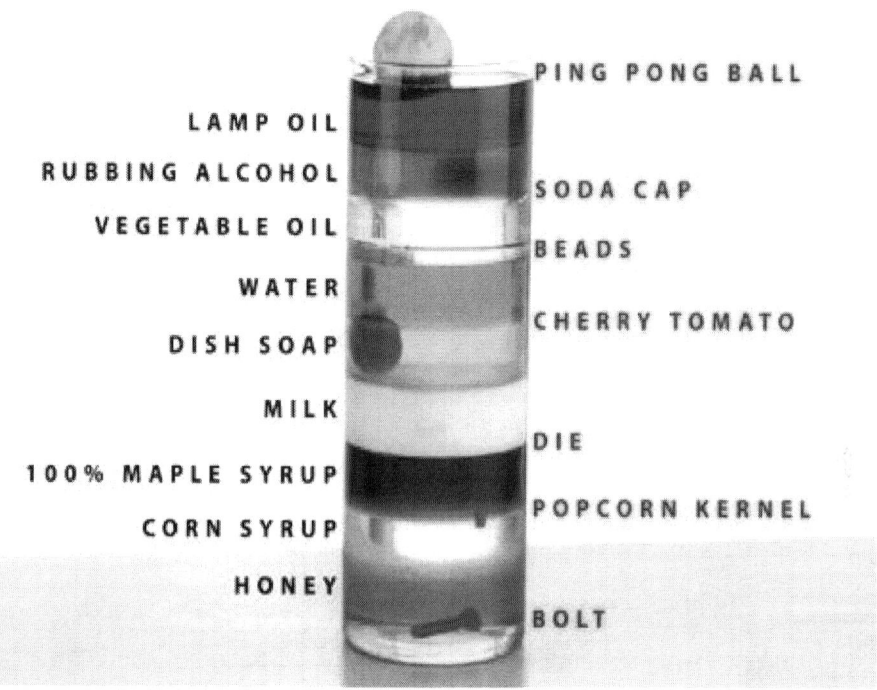

PING PONG BALL
SODA CAP
BEADS
CHERRY TOMATO
DIE
POPCORN KERNEL
BOLT

Dg-striated liquids2

"If you wish to try this at home, alternate layers between hydrophobic/hydrophilic so there is a resistance to mixing at boundaries. Note in the picture the honey, corn syrup and maple syrup are mixing to some extent while the Lamp oil and rubbing alcohol have a crisp border. – Nick"

From http://skeptics.stackexchange.com/questions/11204/is-it-possible-to-stack-liquids-of-different-density-scale-on-top-of-each-other

Creation below the Cosmic Mirror is the domain of the Mother-God, comprised of five levels of conditioned energy. Starting at the bottom, with the lowest-slowest frequency, they are:

Physical (P) or Cellular

Cellular/physical, chemicals and minerals only, the chemical corpse of the human being. Perhaps surprisingly, the home of metabolic activity is not physical but in the lower etheric because metabolism is rhythmic. Nothing is technically alive if we consider only the physical. The physical is only things, only matter, material building blocks. Rocks. Not even what we call "plant life" is wholly physical. Only the dead liquids and fiber of plants are wholly physical. The truly living elements of rocks and plants have their home above the physical; true for animals and humans as well.

(e) lower etheric

This is not a part of the model as given by John-Roger but very much a part of Theosophical and Anthroposophical models. Lower etheric realm. This is the realm of vitality, Chi, and Prana. Acupuncture meridians, health aura and all phenomena related to them are here. Life energy at this level animates the visible physical "corpse" of living beings. The lower etheric is also home to diverse categories of nature spirits, fairies and devas.

Astral (A) or Imaginal

The original Theosophical term was "astral realm." Astral literally means starry. Early clairvoyants were very impressed with the sparkly and colorful quality of the human aura and the appearance of disincarnate beings living on this level, who appear sparkly and colorful. The astral realm is the realm of reactivity, conflict, imagination and ambition. The imaginal realm is also home to many polarities; including, the polarity of "liking and disliking" (Rudolf Steiner 1919). It is the home of the "monkey mind," a common term for excess mental reactivity. It's the home of the animal senses; therefore in people, "fleeting feelings" and "animal passions." It's the homes of one of the energetic "blueprints" of individual human bodies, in their optimal form, shape and structure. It's also populated by Pan, devas, nature spirits, UFOs, aliens; as well as, "Star Trek" and "Federation of Planets" activity, according to UFO experts.

Emotional (C) (Theosophical: Causal realm)

Emotional realm – No longer "fleeting" but "deep emotion;" hence: emotional attachment. Emotional love. Hatred. Theosophists called this the "causal realm" because this realm was viewed as the origin of much of our unresolved causes and effects (karma). This idea dovetails with the more modern idea of emotions as the cause of much of our karma. This dovetails with the idea of emotional attachment as the cause of most of our karma. Theosophy claims this realm is approximately ten times more energetic than any other realm in Creation, at this time. This unfamiliar idea appears abundantly borne out by observation over time: emotions have more "kinetic energy" than other realms at this time.

Mental realm (M)

Mental realm – Form and structure. Beliefs. Mentalizing. Our inner Analyzer. Our inner Critic. Judgment. Evaluations. Allegiances.

Etheric (E), Unconscious or Mythological

This is the Upper etheric realm, the mythological level, home of all Jung's archetypes; including and especially, the divine feminine archetypes; including, the endlessly fertile "Womb of Creation" and Cornucopia.

On the masculine side, the upper etheric is home to the empty void of Zen, the home of "mystery" and "potential" famously characterized as "neither this nor that."

The etheric is home to Goethe's "Ur concepts" and superheroes in their function as caricatures of self-realization.

Moe mundanely, it's also the home of unconscious memories, habits and behaviors, *Scripts People Live* and fairy tales to live by.

The etheric realm is energetic "glue" holding the whole of Creation together. The etheric realm holds all of this Creation together. In each individual person, our etheric body holds all our other bodies into a single unit-identify, giving us the possibility to say, "I am." The upper etheric is the home of the "I am" (comment from Michael Hayes).

The archetypal visual for this is the sphere. At the micro level, in each round animal cell, the etheric is represented by the inner and outer facing cell walls encircling each cell.

If all realms PACME are pictured as bands of liquid, of progressively greater density; then, the Upper Etheric is the least dense, also analogous to the containing glass, holding all of them, making the arrangement coherent, visible, united.

The Etheric has rightly been called the "Web of Life"

and the *Web That Has No Weaver* as it gives sentient beings the felt sense of being one whole rather than disconnected parts.

-=+ -=+ -=+ -=+ -=+ -=+ -=+ -=+ -=+ -=+

End of PACME details

Chapter 3:

How does Spirit view my illness?

When your Guidance is invited to look in on your physical disease, it does not see it as primarily physical. It's easy for Spirit to see very clearly how mental-emotional negativity trickled down and polluted the lower, slower physical body frequency.

Q: Where does physical disease come from?

A: It trickles down from our ACME bodies into our physical body, from our higher frequency bodies, down into our lowest frequency body, our physical-cellular body.

Q: Where are the primary causative factors of illness?

A: Primarily in our ACME bodies. 90% of primary causative agents are INvisible, excepting accidents and trauma medicine.

Q: So if I am only looking at my physical body's illness, I'm only seeing 20% of the total disturbance?

A: 20% of causes found in our physical body is an intelligent guess because we have five bodies. Actually,

the energetic potential of each of our five bodies varies

quite widely. I cannot see this directly myself. Written reports suggest is the energetic potential of our emotional body is perhaps ten times that of the energy potential of our physical body. All our bodies IEMU are more highly energetic than our Cellular body, the Emotional body having the most energy.

This is how and why "little things" like old resentments can take the body down over time; we don't notice them but their negative effect remains powerful on the flesh.

A better guess is 10%. The physical causes of physical diseases is about 10% (John-Roger). What we see of ourselves outwardly here in 3D is about 10% of all the activity and creativity, on all levels, in our psyche (John- Roger).

A humorous way to say this is, down here in 3D, human beings can only see from "I level." Spirit does not have this limitation. If you practice aligning with the Highest Light and Greatest Loving, you will gradually understand how Spirit sees beyond "I level."

Only two kinds of problems

From my point of view as a professional Intuitive, only two kinds of problems exist:

Problems for which you presently have all the primary causative factors accounted for; and,

Problems for which all primary causative factors are not yet in view.

Anyone stuck on a health issue does not yet have all primary causative factors in view yet.

Q: So it's hard to get all the primary cause in view unless and until our IEMU levels are checked?

A: Yes. I have compassion for people who claim this is "backwards" to consider invisible causes more significant than visible causes. It is backwards if materialism is where you are going. However if you are going the other way, trying to "make spirit matter," then the idea of most of the causative factors of our disorders being invisible no longer seems so backwards and inside out.

The paradigm of the Three Selves (basic self, conscious self, high self) and other techniques Medical Intuitives use enlarge the field of inquiry wide enuf to encompass virtually all causative factors. Virtually any physical disturbances will yield its causative factors to analysis within this a field of inquiry enlarged to include IEMU.

Moving within this expanded field is teachable, to those who are looking for this. For instance, the PACME approach to illness and physical pain leads naturally to making a pie chart graph of any illness you wish to address. Call me if you wish to learn this.

Disease are lessons trickling down from ACME into our physical body

Physical diseases and discomforts manifest the same way as anything else manifests in 3D matter, as the last step of a long "rehearsal process."

Before any good idea, a book, a play, a painting, a baby, can manifest in the flesh, it first starts as an Inspiration, an Intuition or an Imagination. Everything here in the physical starts as energy.

From Spirit's point of view, nothing physical can exist in 3D unless and until it has the "scaffolding" of a mental body and an astral body. If our creation is to be alive, it also requires an emotional body and an etheric body of formative forces. This applies to anything living. It applies to you and me. It also applies to germs, diseases and illnesses.

The handful Inspiration-Intuition-Imagination that starts our creative process must clothe itself in slower and lower frequency bodies if we wish it to be visible here in the external 3D world.

First it has to take on archetypal form in the unconscious.

If it then has enuf energy, it can go down to the mental and take on more form and conditioning. If it's a really good idea, it has enuf energy to take on an emotional body and now we have enthusiasm! Only if it still has more energy can it come all the way down into the imagination to be strengthened and energized with ambition, polarity and color. Finally it has to have enuf energy to help the angels give birth to it in physical form.

In this way everything in 3D is the extrusion of creativity down into physical form.

What makes you think disease is any different?

As Spirit looks down on our physical diseases, It does not see them as primarily physical. We see our disease as physical, but we can only see from 'I level.' Spirit does not have this limitation.

It already sees how negativity trickled down from higher frequencies in our psyche down to the lower, slower frequency of our body. In other words, the only way a disease can show in the physical is with a great deal of practice and repetition.

For more discussion of Spiritual Geography and how negativity in our higher frequency bodies pollutes and contaminates our physical bodies, see *You Have Five Bodies, Spiritual Geography 101*.

Q: Why is the outer world more compelling than the inner?

Conventional language for this is found in the topic of introversion and extraversion. Introverts incline more towards our inner world; extraverts incline more towards the outer, external material world.

The West and especially the U.S. is a predominantly extravert culture. Consumerism is virtually 100% about the external world. To get a better balance, we can do with a lot less corporate consumerism.

Achieving a healthy balance of intro- and extra- is one of the chores of a healed K-12 education system.

Waldorf education is the only system of ed I know that comes close.

Excessive material "casts down" our capacity of imagination, persuades it to look only at what can be also felt, tasted, heard and felt. This bias started with the ancient Greeks, from Homer's Odyssey, Book II. the most useful modern translation is, "Better to be a beggar in this world than a king in the land of shades." This has been used to support a wholesale condemnation of anything higher frequency than the physical material world. This bias is now quickly disintegrating, about 50% gone already.

Redeeming the imagination

Ultimately making the inner world more compelling than the outer, in a healthy way, has a lot to do with redeeming the imagination. Again Waldorf-methods education is the only system that seems to understand and put this into action with children. As we redeem our imagination from corporate consumerism, our inner life becomes more interesting. If you can stay in balance, it's possible to imagine how it must be for mystics: the inner more compelling than the outer as a direction for new experiences.

'Willingness to heal' is primarily a phenomena of the inner child If you want to heal and received healing, then you were of one mind. Congratulations!

If you wish to heal and not much happened or you encountered resistance, then you are of two minds.

If you wish to work thru this, you have to explore and come to acknowledge and love your non-dominant mind.

Either the feeling or the thinking mind can be the rational, dominate mind in an individual. In most people in the West, the thinking mind is the rational mind and the feeling mind, in eh gut, is non-dominant, is the "silent partner." We all need to learn to consult our silent partner, our silent teammate, more often. Why? Because without their willingness to change or heal, not much change or healing can take place.

Willingness to change my comfort zone

We each have "comfort zones" on every level of our consciousness, physical-cellular, imaginal, emotional, mental, in our life of unconscious habits.

Because of this, a good definition of growth is upgrading our habits on any level.

Find more discussion in *Your Habit Body, An Owner's Manual*.

Chapter 4:

Reactivity interrupts willingness

Reactivity is a two-edged sword. If we did not react, if you were crossing a street on foot and saw a car bearing down on you, without reactions, you would not have to think, "Now what, if anything, does this have to do with me?"

If our husband smiles and touches our arm in a soft and gentle caress, without reactions we would only be able to think, "Now why is he doing this?" With reactions we move first, think later. Reactivity has its uses. If we are smart, we give them their due and use them to our advantage.

So the game is not to eliminate reactivity but to reduce and moderate EXCESSIVE reactivity, unnecessary reacting to our self other people, the world.

Excess reactivity as excess Liking & Disliking

Reactivity can also be looked at as excess sympathies and antipathies, excess likes and dislikes. Rudolf Steiner suggests the work of growth is largely, "reducing our excess sympathies and antipathies." That's a fair definition of personal growth. It's a precise definition of the big rocks of reactivity to remove first, clearing a path for your own growth.

So, two categories of reacting exist. We may react sympathetically as in, I like it." Or we may react with antipathy, as in, "I don't like it." Ambivalence and confused reactions arise when we have both sympathy and antipathy towards the same thing, like towards Mom, for instance.

With excess sympathy, we react to things favorably even when they are bad for us. The inner child says,

"That chocolate cake would taste so good!"

The conscious yak-yak mind says, "I'm on a diet."

The body, the gut brain says, "But the cake would

taste so good!" We all have parts who lead us to choose behaviors unauthorized or distasteful to our conscious self.

With excess disliking, we react to things unfavorably, even when the thing is healthy. The two year old says, "I hate spinach." The twenty year old says, "I hate putting money in my savings account." The sixty year old says, "I dislike exercising."

Rudolf Steiner's offhand definition of growth as "Overcoming our excess sympathies and antipathies," points to the biggest category of disturbances we have to deal with while on Earth. Until we can get beyond, "I knew it was wrong and I did it anyway," more subtle maturity is elusive. Perhaps the biggest job in self-discipline is to discipline our reactivity.

Being of two minds is a top-bottom split When someone is of two minds, this is never a vertical split but always a horizontal split: The cerebrals nervous system has one point of view; the enteric nervous system is not aligned with the cerebral nervous system; and in fact, has a divergent point of view.

The conscious yak-yak mind says, "I'm on a diet." My body, my gut, my gut brain says, "But the cake would taste so good!" We all have parts who lead us to choose behaviors distasteful to our conscious self.

Reactivity cancels healthy focus

Our the inner child is also our habit body, our capacity to react and to respond subconsciously and unconsciously.

So whenever we are talking about reactions and reactivity, we are talking about the habit body, the inner child, the basic self, etc.

If one part of us is reacting to something other than to our intended goal and dream, then our forces are split. If one part of us has excess liking or excess disliking, these can also pull us out of balance.

Healthy Reactivity is a good thing, excess reactivity, not so much.

Reactivity: "I knew it was bad for me and I did it anyway"

Q: How much excess reactivity do I have?

A: You know you have a lot of reactivity if you find yourself saying, I knew it was bad for me and I did it anyway.

Most of the time, however, we are reacting too quickly to life (John-Roger).

"I knew I shouldn't have eaten it but I ate it anyway."

"I knew I shouldn't have said that but I said it anyway."

"I knew it was bad but I went and did it anyway."

Slowing down our reactions to daily life ~ J-R

Reducing reactivity is the first obstacle we face on a path of personal-spiritual growth.

Q: How far should this slowing down process go?

A: John-Roger once voiced an interesting fantasy, as best I recall it, if you took one day and slowed down your reactions to everything that happened, you might not get much done but you would clear lifetimes of karma.

Reactivity is primarily in the sub-conscious and unconscious levels of the solar plexus (Bertrand Babinet):

subconscious (feeling and desire)
-------------------o--------------------
unconscious (willingness, willfulness, wontfulness, againstness

Healthy & unhealthy exercise of willingness

"Willingness" is a term that benefits terrifically from the qualifiers, "healthy" and "unhealthy." Try it. In many cases, just this resolves 200 years of philosophical confusion.

"Willingness" is the healthy form of "will."

"Will" in the old sense and just about any other expression, is towards the negative, as we shall see.

Chapter 5:

Dysfunctions of Willingness

The origin of conflict and wars is right here. You found it; this is the place.

The word "willpower" becomes mostly useless in a more precise terminology of willingness.

Willfulness is what has created most of our problems here on Earth (Bertrand Babinet).

Let's note it's possible to change and upgrade pockets of willfulness, wontfulness, againstness or resistance you find in yourself.

Redeeming willfulness means locating it in your psyche, upgrading its alignment, aligning this part of your psyche with a higher frequency than the negative it was aligned with prior to your intervention.

This is why so many diverse orgs now use the phrase "for the highest good of all concerned." The idea of a higher good than my mind might conceive of, a continually evolving good as more and more points of view are considered, is indeed the beginning of whole-brained thinking, beginning to penetrate into everyday language.

We only see down here from "I level." Above Island Man, in the high self and higher, Spirit does not have this limitation.

Island Man's narrow-mindedness is by design. Resist

not. Without it, we have no second-order science, the science used for solving exterior problem-solving in the physical-material world.

First-order and third-order sciences, the sciences of the basic self and high self, respectively, are not bound by the "one-eyed, color-blind" vision of Island Man and his second-order science.

Q: If all three parts of our psyche are by design; and, not to be resisted, what's the therapeutic direction for self-healing?

A: To increase our willingness to explore the point of view available to Island Man both above and below him in frequency. Since 1970, this is primarily done by individuals choosing a methods on the Skill Ladder of Holistic Self-Healing methods and techniques and doing their own simple, little experiments. Goethe modeled this in his plant morphology and color experiments before holistic methods and muscle testing were innovate. Rudolf Steiner intuited the value of Goethe's activity; yet, "holism" and "holistic" were not coined until 50 years after his death.

Another therapeutic direction is to recognize Island Man's limited perspective is the perspective of the small "s" ego-self. If you catch yourself making unwanted choices based on this most-limited point of view, you have the right, privilege to re-choose. The human experience affords us opportunity to re-choose, re-choose, re-choose (John-Roger paraphrase).

When willingness "goes bad," dysfunction take several forms:

- denial
- willfulness
- wontfulness
- resistance
- againstness
- doubt
- confusion
- fear

These are all distortions of willingness; they all work against willingness, cancel willingness.

They all block willingness to heal, willingness to be more CIA with the Highest you wish to align with.

Denial blocks willingness to heal. Any kind of denial blocks willingness to heal.

I've had good luck keeping a healing journal on certain issues, rating issues I wish to resolve, on a subjective scale of ten. My goal was to increase my willingness to heal on each issue. My hope was, at the very least, "When the student is ready, the teacher appears." This has worked for me many times. If I prepare, my Universe turns a bit to bring an avenue forward into view.

For me, I work on the issues I have highest willingness to heal first. Only when the inner child is at least somewhat willing and open, can disturbed parts and old habits be balanced, cleared and realigned.

On a scale of ten, I consider 7, 8, 9, 10 "high

willingness." I interpret six or lower to mean I have low willingness to heal. This tells me it's worth looking for where I am of two minds.

The child is mother to the woman

With this in mind, Rudolf Steiner's phrase, "We train the will of children;" can become, "We train the willingness of children." I believe he would approve this change of language. We want the child to have willingness to learn the tools and levers of their local culture; we want children to have willingness toward other people, willingness toward the world and for connecting with their own divinity.

Stephen Colbert's parody of willfulness, wontfulness, resistance & againstness

Stephen Colbert's "stuffed shirt" character makes fun of dysfunctional willingness. He beautifully models willingness gone wrong. On the first Colbert show, available on video, Colbert is surrounded with large stage props with his name in big letters. The big letters throw a shadow of his name on the curtain behind him. His name is on three sides of his desk. Finally his desk, from above, is in the shape of a letter "C." Colbert points to all these and then turns to the audience and says, But this show is not about me--it's about you."

This sense of not-matching, of mismatch, is the source of much humor, a time-honored method used to deflate big egos out of integrity and out of touch with themselves. Colbert makes us laugh at those who cannot release their own self-centered perspective, no matter how urgent the needs of others around them.

The humor here; and also of Randy Martin, of

AskaRepublican.com, is largely based on pointing out where people are of two minds, where they are out of alignment *with themselves* and do not know this, can be in complete denial about being of two minds, about their own internal splits.

Willfulness blocks willingness to heal

It's primarily willfulness that interferes with healthy cooperation between b/s and c/s. The common word is ego, the isolated Decider, the isolated "Unitary Executive," the "lonely robot."

Q: Where is my willfulness?

A: Much of it is in the same place as our "willingness," below the belly button and above the hips, both right and left sides (Merlin & King Arthur).

Q: How do I recognize willfulness?

A: It always has the quality of the ego, not of Light, love and angels. It always has the quality of a downward spiral; instead of, an upward spiral. Its common variations are willfulness, wontfulness, resistance and againstness. These are all distortions of willingness. Check to see if you have againstness towards your self, other people, the world or connecting with your own divinity.

Q: Is willfulness ever good?

A: Perhaps. Compassion Communication favors use of force to protect the innocent from unnecessary harm. If a need exists for justice or fairness, for the highest good of all concerned, then force-willfulness may be justified. "In this situation, I am willing to use force to defend myself;"

Our conscious-waking self has the job of redeeming willingness from where it has fallen into dysfunctional, unhealthy expressions.

Transforming negative habits and expression back to willingness takes only intention, time and attention. Finding my own "lost sheep" in my sub- and unconscious is one of the best uses of my time I'm aware of.

Healthy willingness is gold. Willpower, willfulness, wontfulness, resistance and againstness are unhealthy, rough materials to be transformed. Willingness takes us up; reactivity and willfulness take us down.

The Plan for human beings, in Three Selves terms:

> The high self looks down lovingly on us.
>
> The conscious self looks out lovingly at the world.
>
> The basic self looks up lovingly at the conscious self and high self.

One job of the c/s is to redeem willingness from its dysfunctional expressions. See also: Practitioners: check willingness to heal first!

HealingToolbox.org

Chapter 6:

Where is willingness located in my body?

Willingness, tho invisible is hardly unconditioned. Like personality, willingness has many conditions, determiners and antecedents that become obvious once pointed out.

The short version is both willingness and its dysfunctions are located in your gut brain. That's where to look for it.

Q: Where is my "gut brain"?

A: It's the same as you immune-system-self, mostly below your heart, in the diaphragm area and below to your hips.

John-Roger locates the basic self in his Programming for Multi-dimensional Consciousness, "...just above the belly button or just a little below."

After 15 years of living with J-R's indication, I believe he says 'either above or below the belly button' because in some people, the "center of psychic' gravity in their basic self really is above the belly button, in the area of feeling. For other people, their "center of psychic' gravity in their basic self, is below the belly button, in the area of willingness.

Q: Is there any way to tell by looking at a person or

thru body language whether their basic self is centered more above in "feeling" or below the belly button in "willingness."

A: To some degree yes. You can be tricked but to explore this, watch videos of authentic oriental martial arts masters. You will see a seriousness and groundedness in them. That's what a basic self looks like who is centered and grounded below the belly button. Everything else is towards centeredness above the belly button, many happy children before puberty especially exhibit this.

Either way, above or below, this is where most of our excess reactivity awaits us to be educated.

Reactivity can be conscious, sub- or unconscious, or all three. This is why race-prejudice and gender-prejudice is moderated but not eliminated by governmental rules and laws. The top-conscious part is always the easiest level to clear up. The lower levels challenge your self-awareness and willingness to heal.

I'm pretty sure the following chart is a Bertrand idea, the sub-conscious and unconscious levels of the solar plexus:

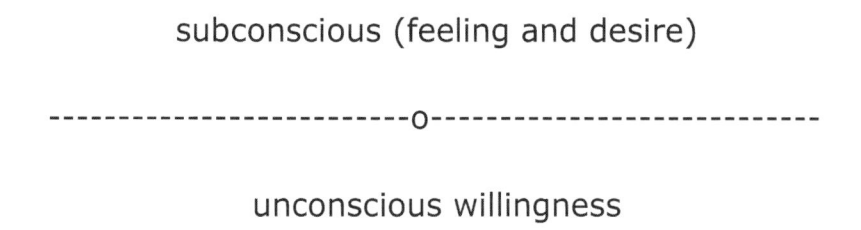

subconscious (feeling and desire)

---------------------------o---------------------------

unconscious willingness

(willfulness, wontfulness, resistance, againstness)

dg-feeling-willingness

The little circle marks your belly button.

The above diagram suggests we have qualitative differences to our reactivity above and below our belly button, feeling and willingness.

The above top~bottom, two-fold model can easily be made into a quadrant system. This is what Bertrand innovated:

Left side	Right side
Mother	**Child**

feeling & desire
---------------------O---------------------
willingness

Grandparent	**Father**
Left side	Right side

dg-inner-family

Diagram of the four quadrants looking down on your own belly button Bertrand evolved his comprehensive and flexible system of the Inner Family.

The four divisions make more personal detail visible than the single term "basic self" or "inner child."

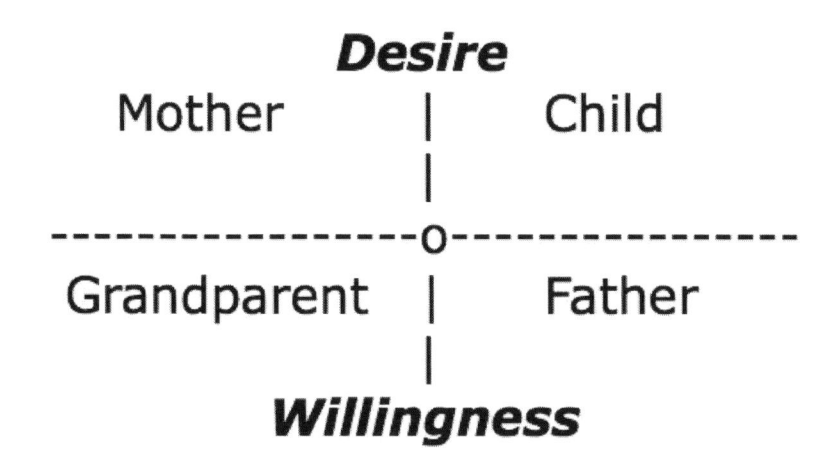

```
              Desire
   Mother       |    Child
                |
   -------------o-------------
   Grandparent  |    Father
                |
             Willingness
```

dg-Inner-Family-feeling-wness2.png

Dg3

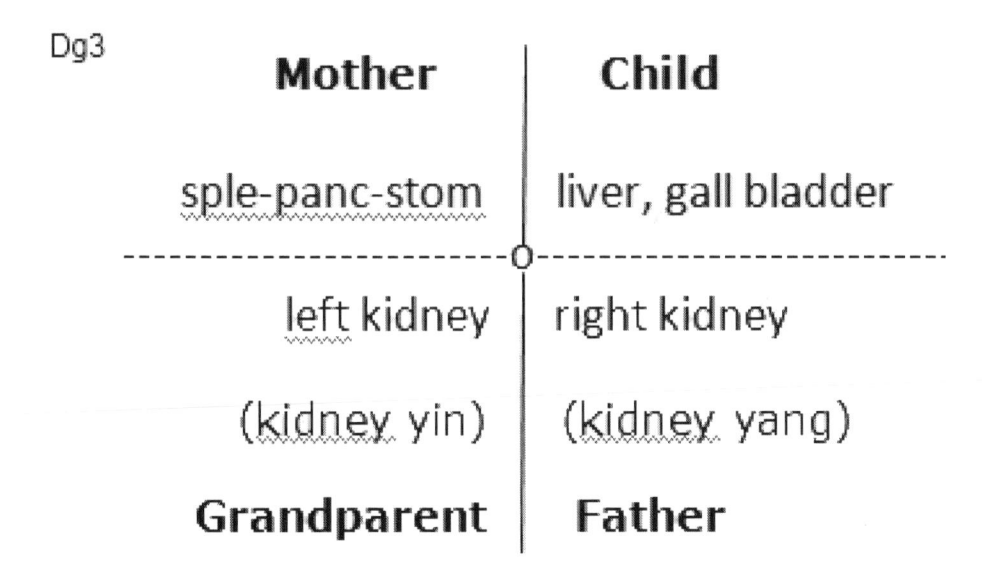

```
         Mother         |    Child

      sple-panc-stom    |    liver, gall bladder
   ---------------------o---------------------
        left kidney     |    right kidney

        (kidney yin)    |    (kidney yang)

        Grandparent     |    Father
```

dg-inner-family-organs3

'Inner Court' innovaiton

In 2001 the present author took the Inner Family further, with an overlay of the archetypes of Arthurian legend:

HealingToolbox.org

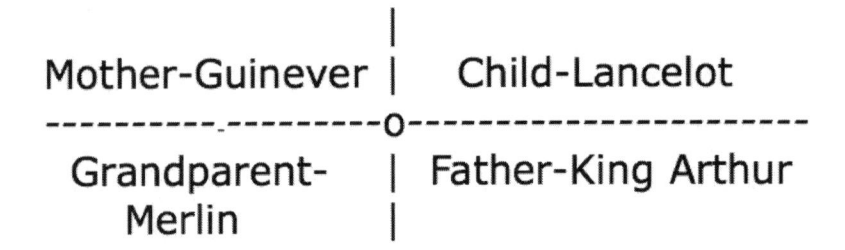

```
              |
Mother-Guinever |   Child-Lancelot
----------.---------O----------------------
 Grandparent-   |   Father-King Arthur
    Merlin     |
```

dg-inner-family-court-gut

The benefit of this overlay is, for those familiar with Arthurian Legend, these names add new dimensions; therefore, a richer, more three-dimensional perception of what is present.

Note how "desire" is now characterized as Guinever-Lancelot and "willingness" is now characterized as Merlin-King Arthur. This has been very useful to me and to clients.

Bertrand characterizes the four quadrants of our gut brain in several additional ways, integrating tradiitonal TCM elemental attributes. One of the most useful is four categories of perceived hurt:

```
        Mother          |         Child
   feeling rejected     |   feeling disappointed
--------------------------O--------------------------
                        |
      Grandparent       |        Father
   feeling abandoned    |    feeling betrayed
```

Dg-inner-family-four-hurts

Willingness is such a crucial aspect of our psyche, the

angels made two places for it in our body, once in the gut brain, the other in the head brain.

The four quadrants of our cerebral brain are explored in *The Inner Court, Close-up of the Habit Body*
https://www.createspace.com/3416651

Chapter 7:

Measuring willingness to heal

Everyone wants to be healed and successful; just ask them. That's us from the neck up.

If I am stuck, not healing, my job is to check myself from the neck DOWN, check my child within.

Measuring willingness to heal in my child within; as in, "What is MY willingness to heal?" Is where most people will want to start.

You do NOT need muscle testing to begin testing yourself. Muscle testing only makes testing yourself faster, easier and more precise, for most people.

Subjective testing will feel like guessing--that's fine.

To do this exercise, please pick something you wish to heal or clarify.

I found a way for people to make useful distinctions, that is simplicity itself.

Two measures, one from neck-up, another from neck-down

Try making two measurements, one from the neck up, the other from the neck down.

From the neck up represents the interests-desires of your waking-conscious self about healing your target.

Two measures are needed because we have TWO lower selves. They are designed to work as teammates, partners.

Virtually all success literature prior to 2014 fails to make this distinction, forgetting we have a second, silent partner, who needs to be on board with our goals and projects; AND, that its participation CAN BE MEASURED.

Measuring from the neck up and the neck down is also useful because most people are vey poor guessers about what their child within is up to. Deliberately and consciously testing remedies this vagueness and dreaminess. We want more accurate inner pictures of who is doing what inside us, right?

Measuring above and below the neck gives us more accurate pictures and encourages us to be curious, which is very helpful, compared to vague guessing and assumptions.

If this first number is high--and your concern remains unresolved, you can now measure your willingness to heal--on the identical concern--from the neck down.

Please DO THIS NOW. Get a second person to assist you if you need assistance.

Examples.

A client wanted to measure how open she was to her husband. She was very surprised to learn that she was more open to her husband below the neck than above the neck. This "upset her apple cart" in a very productive way, leading to her reassessing how much her own fear and mentalizing were factors in the gap between her and her husband.

Q: Egad! My willingness to heal neck-down is very different! What do I do?

A: This is normal and average. It simply means your rational mind has one view of healing your concern; and, your inner child has another view.

This demonstrates how I am "of two minds" on my desire to heal?

This is how our energetic strength is split, slowing our movement towards our goals-projects.

Q: How do I increase my willingness to heal?

A: We increase willingness to heal simply by asking for it, setting our intention to heal our target issue. Why? Asking is a soul action. Attention and intention are soul actions.

Affirmations can be useful; but only, if the old junk has already or at least mostly been taken out and subtracted. Most of our karma is cleared thru subtraction. Subtraction before addition, in self-healing, always, here. Slow-Motion Forgiveness (TM) is one tool for this.

So if you have taken out the guilt, remorse, judgments, etc, affirmations are the main additive process. One place they come into play is when willingness to heal is low.

Repeating what you want more of, and tapping around your belly button can wake up your enteric nervous system to get on board the train.

Exercise any intention, especially on a daily basis, and your silent partner will likely follow along sooner or later.

Q: Can I measure my own willingness to heal?

A: Yes. The best ethics are each person measures only for them self.

If you use dowsing or self-test some how, go for it! Or you can find a friend to pull your arm down while YOU ask the question and YOU evaluate the response, not them. Don't let anyone play expert to your own inner world. You are the Once and Future Queen in your inner life and no one else. You be the expert on you. Let no one rob you of your experience.

Q: What if I don't trust my own self-testing?

A: Three ways come to mind.

1) Take a step back. Have a second person pull your arm down and you evaluate results until you can get the same answer to the same question three days in a row. Build up your self-confidence from there.

2) The book *Self-Healing 101!* Has seven safe, gentle and effective invitations to communicate with your own Little Artist.

3) A Muscle Testing Practice Group DVD is available. It address difficulties in testing.

༶

Chapter 8:

To all practitioners: check willingness to heal FIRST in your sessions

One of my most useful learnings from ten years of working with clients has been to check the client's willingness to heal--early and often. For practitioners, willingness to heal is the pre-requisite for ALL healing sessions. Only as the inner child is willing and open, can unresolved disturbances emerge, be matched with remedies, be released; and, energies formerly tied up in negativity, be realigned with Love, Light and Angels.

The biggest muddles I get into with healing myself and clients is mistaking, "Yes, I want to work on that," with a high willingness to heal.

The fact is, unless high willingness to heal is present, seven out of ten, 7/10, or higher, the inner child is not ready to move energy towards wellness--no matter what the rational mind wants.

We waste a lot of time in self-healing when we forget self-healing requires the cooperation and alignment of our habit body with the stated goal of the conscious self.

If sessions are begun on issues where the willingness to heal in the inner child is low, these sessions can meander around aimlessly.

Even if I do wonderful, accurate detective work, often client feel, "nothing happened." Same for when I work on myself and ignore low willingness to heal in my own Inner Healer.

My goal in every session now is to ascertain, by measuring on a scale of 1-10, how willing the inner child is to heal the disturbance I have in mind.

The relevance of willingness to healing is demonstrated in health practices of every kind. No healing takes place unless a willingness to heal is present.

How I used to do sessions

With clients and myself, it's common to find my rational mind saying, "Yes, I want to heal X." However, when I ask the basic self, I find less alignment with the intention to heal.

This means the client is of two minds. They may not know this.

The basic self below the diaphragm muscle, a person's habit body, has to be "on board" and aligned with a clearing action before much movement will take place in a client session.

In the old days with patrons, I simply asked them, "What do you want to work on?" I asked this because the more they can narrow their "energetic target" the better the session goes.

Sessions sometimes became problematic. No matter how hard or well I worked, there was little energetic shift for the client. If I dug deeper, I got better results from my point of view but client's only said, "Eh, I don't feel much." So even if I did wonderful energetic work, often the patron felt "nothing happened."

These problematic situations ended when I began assessing the client's willingness to heal on their target issue FIRST.

I learned while the client's conscious self may say, "Yes, I want to heal (target X)," when I asked their basic self if it was in agreement, also wished to heal target X, I found the inner child was NOT so inclined; it was not in alignment with the intention to heal target X. It had another idea and interest entirely!

Gradually I came to understand this unpacks the common phrase, "be of two minds." 90% of clients have no idea this is happening, that their forces are split, half of their healing team, the immune system, is not on board for healing what the mind wishes to heal.

The basic self below the belly button is the home of willingness. This part has to be "on board" and aligned with a clearing action for much movement to take place in a 1:1 session. I find the b/s has to be at a 6/10 willingness to heal or better for me to feel confident that good movement can take place in a session.

If the client says I want to clear up X and the willingness to heal is 7/10 or higher, then the basic self is also willing to cooperate with that shift as well.

If the client says, I want to clear up X and the willingness to heal is 6/10 or lower, then the c/s and b/s are not in concert on what to heal.

Make sense?

Only as the inner child is at least somewhat willing and open, can disturbed parts and old habits be balanced. In sessions with patrons, the degree of change achieved, as perceived by the patron, appears to have 90% to do with their willingness to heal, not with the skill of the practitioner. If you are ready to heal, almost anyone can assist you.

Case study: How I do sessions now

A client comes to me and says, "Bruce I want to work on losing weight. I've tried everything. Why am I so heavy?"

I say, "Great! That's a clear target; you know what you want. Let's check with your inner child and learn her willingness to heal on your goal."

I check with K-testing and her willingness to heal in the inner child is only 2/10.

So I tell the client, "You are of two minds. Your conscious self wants one thing but your inner child has something else in mind."

So we talk. I don't want to work until her conscious self and inner child BOTH have agreement on what to heal. I need them to be a team, working together on one goal, the same goal.

Either we find an approach to the target they both want; or, we explore what is bothering the inner child and make that the priority.

In the second case, shifting to what the inner child wants to clear, we hear the inner child is carrying the extra weight as part of a personal protection routine.

I ask her inner child, "What is your willingness to reducing unconscious protection routines?" The inner child has 9/10 willingness to heal the issue of reducing protection patterns. The client takes great strides forward in the session because now the c/s and inner child are on the same page; they both want the same thing resolved.

Then what happens when we work now? The client STRIDES forward in the session because the c/s and inner child are on the same page; they both want the same thing resolved; they both have the same target.

The fact is, unless high willingness to heal is present, six out of ten, 6/10, or higher, the inner child is not ready to move energy towards wellness--no matter what the conscious self wants.

Clients return for repeat business with practitioners based on their perception of movement and results. Their willingness to heal has as much or more to do with how much movement takes places in a session as the skill of the practitioner. In other words, if you are ready to heal, strongly motivated to move energy, almost anyone can assist you.

Q: How do I raise my willingness to heal?

A: This is very easy to do and is one of the good uses of affirmations, adding in an intention where previously there was nothing.

Words we speak aloud, especially if we speak with coherence, integration and alignment, impacts our sub and unconscious very strongly. Your words are nothing to sneeze at. To help clients raise a low willingness to heal, I will ask them to say "I want to heal my _____" out loud so we can get enuf openness in the deeper levels to see what's going on.

Q: Does this happen in self-healing as well?

A: you bet. The dynamic of being of two minds, the blocks healing, is equally present in self-healing. Difficult to work on your own issues if your thinking mind and feeling mind are not together on what to shift

Q: What if I don't know what my basic self wants?

A: The conscious self does not have to know; it only has to ASK. That's what K-testing is so useful for.

HealingToolbox.org

If one self has low willingness to heal, I slow down and we try to get the cerebral and enteric nervous system both on the same page, seeing the same goal and both agreeing it's a desirable and beneficial goal.

The conscious and basic selves do not need to be 100% in alignment. This is rare so don't expect it.

If the basic is NOT in concert on healing the target, then you are back to listening and negotiation. Find an issue the basic and you both wish to heal!

The moral of this story is: check willingness to heal first.

The greater the combined willingness to heal of cerebral and enteric nervous systems, the easier the healing goes and the more dramatic the results are likely to be.

Q: Why does the lower self have different goals from the conscious self?

A: We have "comfort zones" on every level of our psyche.

Our comfort zones are the way we are used to doing things. Our inner operating system clings to the familiar and predictable way of doing things on all levels, physically, imaginatively, emotionally, mentally and unconsciously.

Healing and growth always impacts our habit body.

Healing and growth are well-defined as upgrading our

habit body on any level.

This is true for "change" as well: Willingness to change is the prerequisite to all change. To change or alter our habits requires attention, intention and courage. For human beings, you CAN "teach an old dog new tricks;" it simply takes more effort to re-direct them than pups who are empty of programming!

Q: Why should I test myself for "Willingness to heal" first?

A: You may not know you are of two minds until you test.

It's no crime to be two minds. It simply means you have an area where you could be more Coherent, Integrated and Aligned (CIA) if you wish to be.

This has to be done right at the start, as soon as a patron announces what issue they wish to work on. Then—is the inner child aligned with the conscious self? Test how aligned the inner child is with the goal stated by the conscious self and you have a preview of how much "momentum" the patron has to heal on that issue.

The moral of this story is: check willingness to heal first.

If you are a practitioner, make sure the feeling mind of your patron is in agreement on the announced goal. The greater a patron's willingness to heal, the easier the healing and the more dramatic results are likely to be.

Q: What constitutes "high willingness to heal"?

A: Numbers are an easy way to quantify things for the c/s, so we can work with them. Remember tho, the feeling comes first, the number simply measures the feeling.

Chapter 9:

Where's my magic pill?

I want to be healed NOW!

Managing your expectations

The ego always wants a free lunch. It wants to hear, "I'll give you this magic pill/treatment/electric device instrument/ exercise/technique and your suffering will go away.

Why is this so unlikely? Because our illnesses are not one thing.

Like a master oil painting, our illnesses are built up from many layers and fields of color put on the canvas, overlapping fields. For a disturbance to manifest in the physical, we have already laid down many earlier layers in the imaginal, emotional, mental and unconscious levels of our "canvas."

Understanding does not count for as much as our mind would like to think, "Whatever you think the cause of the problem is-that's not the cause," says USM.

One reason for this is it's difficult for the conscious-waking self to assign responsibility to itself for things-gone-wrong.

Q: Why is this?

A: Because our waking conscious self is embarrassed it has so few Tools That Heal to deal with things like physical illness. It's embarrassing to our small "s" ego self. Who likes facing their own weakness, their own definite? Only the strong, perhaps.

Our small "s" ego self wants to blame someone else, if it thinks it can get away with it. Island Man wants someone else to take the fall: poor hygiene, bacteria, viruses, genes, cancer, etc.

This excuses the c/s from responsibility for its poor choices and/or ignorance. It's not popular to admit disease often results from long sequences of poor choices I have made. Well, it's unpopular everywhere but in healing groups and people interested in the original impulse of psychosomatic medicine and among Heroes of Self-healing.

Pathology-pharmacology-oriented doctors collude with patients to excuse them from its natural responsibility. Few doctors have the counseling skills to put patients at ease so patients can hear the message, "Your past choices and ignorance led to this physical result." Conventional medical and pharmaceutical industries make more income if patients believe external causes are the culprit and can be controlled with this drug or that machine.

The ego likes to feel, "I'm still in control." The mood of extraverted thinking, invoking external cause and effect is very comforting to the isolated conscious self. Then everything is kept exterior and at the mental level, in the light of day, and we can focus on material things, like bacteria and virus-instead of our unhealthy choices.

Problem is, few diseases other than broken bones and infections are primarily physical in origin. Virtually all chronic diseases appear to be primarily invisible in origin, though physical complications do, er, complicate matters.

I once heard in a metaphysical circle the angels guiding humankind were happy when 18th century minds began discussing and experimenting with cause and effect. Then when 19th century minds limited cause and effect to only the physical-material plane alone, ignoring emotional and mental cause and effect, the angels began to cry.

Learning cause and effect in the mind and emotions remains a big lesson on Earth today.

Chapter 10:

Other things you can measure

Q: Self-measuring seems like it might have more uses. Does it?

A: Yes, for those who are looking for it.

'Willingness to heal' is only one of several useful measures of willingness I have found. Decades ago I went to a healer named Bill Stratton, who now lives in San Diego.

As part of his intake process he measured me in these dimensions:

> My willingness to serve
>
> My willingness love
>
> My willingness to learn

A worksheet on this could be:

> What is your willingness to serve here on Earth? = ___/10
>
> What is your willingness to love here on Earth? = ___/10
>
> What is your willingness to learn and gain wisdom here on Earth? = ___/10

If you ask any person off the street these questions, they say, "Of course I want to; I'm a 10/10 or higher."

So some practice and discrimination is needed to learn when you are accessing responses from your own silent partner living in Theta and Delta; and when, you are simply accessing your own opinion, from the neck-up. Your own opinion, you already know. Accessing the response of your silent partner can be a surprise.

HealingToolbox.org

See more discussion of the difference between neck-up and neck-down in *You Have Three Selves* and *Muscle Testing as a Spiritual Exercise*.

Your Ring of Success is made up of six links

Q: What about measuring success?

A: Success Kinesiology is a good name for muscle testing, self-testing applied to success issues. It became a whole book, out now.

Anyone who wishes to can ask, "What is my willingness to be successful here in the 3D world?"

As long as you clearly measure your self BELOW the neck, from the neck-down, you'll learn how aligned your child within is with your conscious-waking success goals.

This protocol evolved into the Success Profile, an initial gift session by phone-Skype available to anyone who has not already worked with me professionally.

It's only ethical for me to measure your links if, once we find it, I can also strengthen your weakest link. The testing parts takes about two minutes. I hope you will learn to do this yourself.

Let's make friends, family and especially green-holistic practitioners and entrepreneurs as successful as possible! PLEASE duplicate and experiment with this form, with 'God as your Partner:'

1) Willingness to have money and own material things: _____/10

2) Willingness to engage with people, be successful with people: _____/10

3) Willingness to be self-supporting here in the 3D world: _____/10

4) Willingness to assist other people with their goals, dreams and passions: _____/10

5) Willingness to partner with my own child within in my 3D success: _____/10

6) Willingness to chunk down both goals and issues into bite-sized pieces: _____/10

6) Willingness to partner with my own Divinity in my 3D success: _____/10

Q: What if I get a low number? How do I raise it?

A: A Healing Coach can show you how. I have a mentor I see regularly. Do you?

Raising your own low number is easy to do in person or by phone but complex to explain in print.

Q: How can I learn more Tools That Heal?

A: When much new language is needed all at once, we go to a school to learn the new ideas and how they fit together. HealingToolbox.org is one place offering people new Tools That Heal, one-on-one sessions and live classes.

Four categories of human issues in Book of Genesis

This also comes from Bertrand Babinet. I really did find the page in Genesis where it mentions the four categories of human issues. If you know the chapter and verse, please send it in, not so easy to find.

Our unconscious issues may be invisible yet they are still highly patterned. These patterns can be known and shifted, using the Light. It turns out it's quite difficult to find a life issues that does NOT fall into one of these four categories:

> Issues with your self
>
> Issues with other people
>
> issues with the world
>
> issues with God

Let's unpack these a bit so you can make use of them.

> Issues with your self: health, with your own inner child.
>
> Issues with other people: mother, father, wife, husband, friends, tribe, lovers co-workers, people you know
>
> Issues with the world: people you don't know (potential clients-customers), career, money and service.

Issues with God: bosses, authority in any form including how you connect with your own Divinity, the Home Office.

Feel free to make your own longer list of these categories.

Issues with God and your own Divinity

This is clearly the most mysterious category. This is only because of the atheistic times we live in, relative to our human potential Because secular and ecumenical language for our issues with God is so rare, I often have to do some explaining to people so they can make a connection when their disturbances tracks back to this category of human issues.

See if any of these are familiar to you:

- feeling abandoned by God

- feeling betrayed by God

- feeling disappointed by God

- feeling rejected by God

- addiction and attachment to religious ritual obscuring the Beloved

- prior history with spiritual groups

- anger at God (Including: Why do bad things happen to good people?)

Possible additional major categories

In my experience, occasionally an issue does not test into one of the four categories. I usually chalk this up to my shortcomings as a tester. Additional work-arounds, that may lead to uncovering the category, can be:

- Trauma and often the trauma is...

- A hidden, cloaked or disguised issue

- Not safe to go there. Check if the issue is safe to raise.

The inner child may have a ban, a prohibition on airing it.

- A competency you never learned in this or any lifetime.

Chapter 11:

Willingness in groups and group process

Willingness and the consensus process

Roberts Rules of Order (RRO) is the playbook and

rulebook for majority rule in patriarchal groups. Its rules are based on the assumption of conflict and competing points of view. RRO assumes robust and healthy dialog arises out of conflict. In a competitive male context, RRO is stupendous. You can hear RRO used in virtually any City Council or School Board meeting today.

Again, RRO assumes conflict and competing points of view; this is the given. But what about a group who already share many values and want to expand their consensus?

In the RRO model, robust, healthy, productive decisions is the goal of dialog. When it works, when decisions are made satisfactory to all parties, we have the positive of Marx & Hegel's dialectic clash of opposing ideas and the ensuring synthesis.

True to its roots in patriarchy, RRO is a "winner take all" model, only ONE view can win.

In RRO, if the topic is Creationism vs. Evolution, there cannot be both. There is only never killing any human fetus. Or there is abandoning a fetus at any time for any reason. RRO favors black and white formulations.

High contrast between values is no longer so helpful when the will towards consesnus is already strong, where both reconciliation and negotiation are desired by the majority.

Planet Earth can no longer sustain "Every man for himself competition." Culturally speaking, competition, the competitive paradigm, is a walking corpse.

Cooperation is the norm now. Earth cul;ture is way behind on this since "inner cooperation" is realtively rare, except in circles around holistic coches and healers.

These orgs have already turned 180 degrees from assuming competition to assuming cooperation. Now it's time for more orgs to practice this change. Those who do, will have longevity pst the coming Transiiton.

When old orgs unable to make the Transiiton to truly human values, new orgs will replace them, run by plain folks like you and me, willing to listen, learn and honor each other as 'hearts in the making.'

RRO is passe for another reason. If you listen to City Council or School Board meetings, alert observers notice feelings and needs are rarely ever mentioned.

No place for them at a City Council meeting, you say?

Notice without mention of feelings and needs the whole affect, the emotional quality of a meeting is dull and lifeless.

This also identifies the problem we have more generally in politics and civic life: meetings are no fun so few people attend.

Roberts Rules of Order (RRO) hangs on today anywhere men subscribe--unconsciously--to domination as a value; and, believe the only two choices available are demanding in anger or submission; so, better not be on the submitting end of a negotiation. As long as forcing-coercing the minority to either rebel or submit to majority rule, we are in either-or, black and white thinking, in Patriarchy, not yet learning from Nonviolent Communication.

So what replaces Robert Rules of Order?

Blueprint of WE is a new process for making agreements with yourself and/or with other people, more aligned with feminine values and Compassionate Communication (NVC). It's also known as: "State of Grace."

Blueprint of WE assumes interpersonal conflict is not an "IF" but a "WHEN." Hence, the goal is anticipating and reducing conflict as it will arise and must be prepared for.

Main site has 15 pdfs you can download for free: http://www.blueprintofwe.com/

Many videos: Here's the left brain one: http://www.youtube.com/watch?v=y8rfVxltwGY

Very artistic right-brain joyful presentation here: http://www.youtube.com/user/CollaborativelyAware

Blueprint of WE is a simple, grassroots, process for making agreements with yourself and/or with other people.

Where "lawyerese" contract language supports and enforces masculine-patriarchal values, Blueprint of WE aligns with and supports practical feminine values in partnerships and in the work place.

You can also work the process with only yourself, for specific challenging tasks.

The Blueprint of WE process leads people to conversation and consensus on:

- WHAT the agreement is,

- WHAT the BENEFITS are for each person,

- HOW to DEFUSE CONFLICTS likely to arise around it.

This way Blueprint of WE is a collaborative tool for building trust, respect sustainability within:

- your self, inner cooperation

- partnerships of any kind,

- business orgs

- communities

A Blueprint of WE document is preventative maintenance, a modern way to establish foundations of mutual trust and respect, thru a custom-designed set of guidelines for heightening awareness of interpersonal conflict, at the bud or baby stage; and, how to address it early on. It is perhaps of greatest value for groups attempting to build or sustain a collective vision.

It could be used to bring greater cohesion within an existing face-to-face group or Board by creating greater, more durable interpersonal connections.

Similarly, it could easily be employed to facilitate one-to-one understanding between TFH practitioners, holistic clinic staff and for composing joint ventures between TFH members and the Board. Blueprint of WE could be a powerful communication tool within our Board and between TFH members.

Main site has 15 pdfs you can download for free: http://www.blueprintofwe.com/

Many videos: Here's the left brain one: http://www.youtube.com/watch?v=y8rfVxltwGY

Very artistic right-brain joyful presentation here: http://www.youtube.com/user/CollaborativelyAware

This Tool That Heals was brought to my attention by a Touch for Health member, Bruce Dickson, in L.A.. I see why he believed it could be applicable to the Touch for Health Kinesiology Association.

It resonates with me because of it's far-reaching usefulness and focus on solidifying existing or new relationships, anywhere consensus between people is desired. It can even be taken home for use in the home between our loved ones--just like Touch for Health

Quieting the "safety brain"

Blueprint of WE is a conflict prevention tool, a conflict anticipation tool. Anticipating the inevitability of conflict, Blueprint of WE, prepares all parties involved with what to do when conflict appears in any party to the agreement. Thus, "quieting the safety brain."

"Collaborative awareness" vs. "self awareness"

The two woman founders identify a need to move beyond me-me-me into collaborative awareness. Blueprint of WE is working smart and working practical, from a feminine perspective. It facilitates groups of self-aware people to clarify and maintain alignment when playing together.

FIVE Components of Blueprint of WE

(Revised for clarity from their thumbnail online)

1. The Story of Us

1. What draws you to consider this agreement, to work with these people - to this situation - this task - project? These are the benefits you are looking for, your expectations and assumptions. Get all these out on the table.

2. Interaction Styles ~ How I work best, what I look like on a good day.

3. Warning Signs ~ What I look like on a bad day. What I might need that you can ask me, that I may be unable to ask myself, in the moment. For example, "Is there something preventing you from being present you'd like to talk about?"

4. "Red flags" to your continued participation. Non-negotiable "show stoppers" that will cause you to stop participating. The structure and the ethics you require to create and sustain participation in this agreement-project-task.

5. Questions you can ask me (I can ask myself) to Return to Peace, if I'm out of balance. Makes the difficult times shorter and easier. Re-negotiation preferences. Put on the table questions people can ask you when you appear out of balance to them; such as, "What are you needing now?"

6. How long you're willing to go before you make peace or address a conflict. Five minutes? A day? Agreements of non-violence. Statements about worst case scenarios if the unimaginable happens. Willingness to keep an open mind, if "show stoppers" in (4) occur.

- See more at: http://www.blueprintofwe.com/whatisit.html#sthash.CbKV1T0i.dpuf

There is a nice intro video at their website www.blueprintofwe.com.

Downloadable PDF of how to create a document at http://www.blueprintofwe.com/learnmore.html#downloadablematerials

Willingness and living NOW

As some readers will intuit, healthy willingness is highly connected with living a 'spirit-led life.'

This new language connects with old language, I think, of the Christian hermits of the first couple hundreds years after Christ. One of their ideals was later known as "poverty, chastity and obedience."

Imagine how much willingness it take sot live that way

and have it meet all your needs; it's a lot!

We can also point to the connection between willingness and living in the NOW. All those Zen koans about giving up the mind...

The Plan for human beings

>The high self looks down lovingly on us.
>
>The conscious self looks out lovingly at the world.
>
>The basic self looks up lovingly at the conscious self and high self.

Willingness and children

Rudolf Steiner's phrase, "We train the will of children" becomes today, "We train the willingness of children." I believe he would approve this upgrade of his language.

We want the child to have willingness to take care of them self on all levels, willingness to connect with other people, willingness to express their uniqueness here in the 3D world and to make the world a better place, and willingness to connect with their own Divinity and exercise a life of aspiration.

Willingness is the key to aligning and integrating the three selves. Willingness is where the whole topic of the 3S leads.

To Learn More:

Forgiveness, the Key to the Kingdom by John-Roger. This book has virtually no "how to" on forgiveness; still, any page you turn to has the frequency of forgiveness, a terrific touchstone.

Initial gift phone-Skype sessions between 8 AM and 9:00 PM PST only.

Phone 310-280-1176 ~ Skype: SelfHealingCoach

More topics like this at http://www.HealingToolbox.org

About the Author

Bruce has a series of 16 books, 20 videos and 200 articles on Best Practices in Energy Medicine. Find him at HealingToolbox.org

Bruce co-founded the Holistic Chamber of Commerce in Los Angeles.

Health Intuitive Bruce Dickson shows people how to use their own Inner Dashboard so they can increase their own Inner Sunshine. How? By identifying and removing blocks and obstacles to health and success.

Many ways to connect with your own Guidance exist

thru the Skill Ladder of Holistic Self-healing Techniques-Methods-Arts. Everyone who wants to can use Tools That Heal and apply Best Practices in Holistic Self-Healing.

Tools That Heal Press Booklist

Best Practices in Holistic Self-Healing Series

Resources written by and for self-testers

In all modalities

Tools That Heal composed by and for self-healers and self-muscle-testers in all therapeutic modalities.

HealingToolbox.org ~ 310-280-1176 ~ Gift sessions by phone to find and repair the weak link in your Ring of Success. Practitioners, healers and coaches especially invited to call.

All books written in an interactive, FUN style by a practicing Health Intuitive with training from MSIA, USM, NVC and Waldorf teacher training from Rudolf Steiner College.

All books available in PAPER and EBOOK.

Best Practices in Holistic Self-Healing Series

The two best sellers:

3) Meridian Metaphors, Psychology of the Meridians and Major Organs

HealingToolbox.org

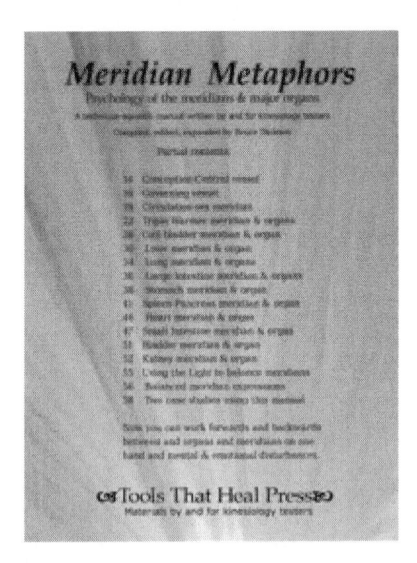

Ever wonder what the connection between meridians, organs and emotions is? Ever think TCM had a start on good ideas but much was missing? Now anyone can work either forwards or backwards, between disturbed organs and meridians on one hand; and, disturbed mental-emotional states on the other hand. All descriptions begin with healthy function. Disturbances are further categorized by under- and overcharge conditions. Includes the myths and metaphors of under- overcharged organs-meridians condensed from Psychological Kinesiology plus much new material from other clinical practitioners. 22,000 words 100 page manual, 8 x10"

11) *The NEW Energy Anatomy:*

Nine new views of human energy that don't require clairvoyance

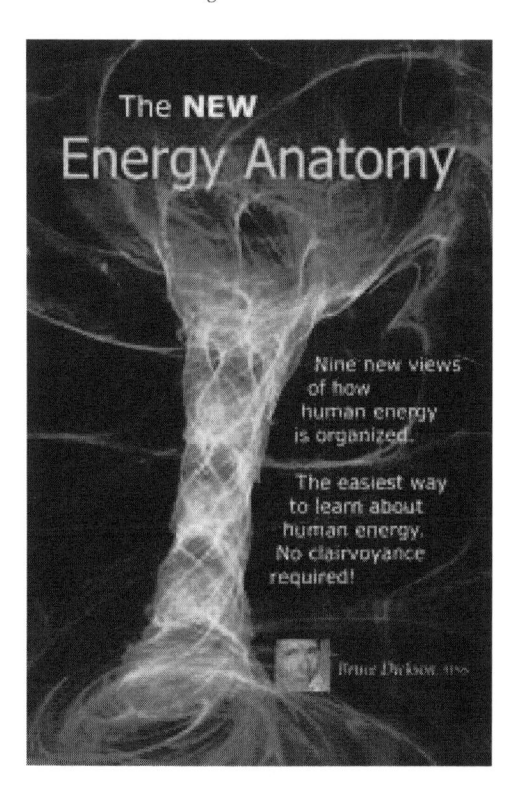

The Three Selves is simply the clearest, easiest map-model for the whole person. Here's the greater detail you would expect in an anatomy that goes with the 3S.

An easier, simpler, faster way to learn about human energy system compared to the chakra system. The NEW Energy Anatomy is a better entry point for students to developing sensitivity. Each view is testable with kinesiology of any and all kinds. You be the judge!

Physical anatomy is used by every effective energetic practitioner and self-healer. When your target is invisible, as often true--the best map is invaluable!

Maps of chakras, auras, acupuncture points, and reflex

points are common—and commonly confusing to students because they cannot be perceived directly without clairvoyance. If you ARE clairvoyant, these aspects are easier to perceive and lead into the even deeper symbology of the chakra system.

These nine simpler views replace the chakra system as a starting place for most students of human energy. Each one is testable with kinesiology of any method. See for yourself!

NEW Energy Anatomy replaces some of the older views of human energy with views much simpler to visualize

Particularly useful for energy school students and sensitive persons using testing to sort out their abundant perceptions. More generally useful for efforts to become more Coherent, Integrated and Aligned (the new CIA). Coupled with Touch for Health, EFT, Energy Medicine or PTS Masters and Doctorate programs, these views facilitate making your aura brighter.

Human energy is organized:

1) Right and left in the body, yin & yang in the body.

2) Top and bottom, enteric and cerebral nervous systems.

3) Front and back, CV-GV, Clark Kent and Superman.

4) As frequency, best viewed as four kinds of laughter!

5) Our gut brain has two frequencies, divided top and

bottom, feeling above (hey, hey hey!) and willingness below (ho, ho, ho!).

6) Our inner child has four distinct quadrants, an Inner Court.

7) We have a second Inner Court in our head.

8) The back of our head is willingness to heal our past.

9) Hip stability is a Ring of Loving you can strengthen.

Other material includes the Law of Gentleness for healers, coaches & counselors. 25,000 words 145 p. in 6x9 format.

1) **You have FIVE bodies, PACME, Spiritual Geography 101** (99 cent eBook)

You have FIVE bodies PACME
Spiritual Geography 101

Bruce Dickson, MSS, MA

Tools That Heal Press
Best Practices in Self-Healing System Series
HealingToolbox.org

A fundamental distinction John-Roger and others make early and often is the useful tool of Spiritual Geography, discerning we have not one body here on Earth, but FIVE. Take away or compromise with any one of these bodies and we become less than fully human, less than fully capable of giving and receiving love. Topics include:

What makes us human is primarily invisible

Experience your five bodies RIGHT NOW

Two simple spiritual geographies

The map of Creation in your own hand

PACME ~ low frequency to high frequency

HealingToolbox.org

Tiger's Fang & When Are You Coming Home?

PACME can also be concentric circles

We have habits and comfort zones on each level PACME

Can I measure the soul here in 3D?

Can I see the soul here in the 3D world?

How does Spirit view my illness?

Where does physical disease come from?

Where are the primary causative factors of illness?

Only two kinds of problems

Why is the outer world more compelling than the inner?

Redeeming the imagination

2) The Meaning of Illness is Now an Open Book;
Cross-referencing Illness and Issues

Virtually unknown to the public, EIGHT excellent, peer-reviewed books exist correlating illnesses and mental-emotional issues as of 2013.

It's now possible to simply look up the meaning of physical illnesses, the causative issues behind health concerns. Some combination of these mental-emotional issues is what oppresses your organs, tissues and cells.

For persons with their own Healing Toolbox, they can simply get busy doing what you can to locate, address and resolve these issues. Muscle testing, kinesiology testing of any kind is the most convenient way to navigate to which issue is "live" in you.

If you don't know where your Healing Toolbox is or what's in it, you can always find a Self-Healing Coach, Health Intuitive or Medical Intuitive. Find someone who works with loving.

Those interested in the mental-emotional meaning of illnesses tend to be, self-healers, self-muscle-testers, holistic practitioners, kinesiology practitioners, Medical and Health Intuitives, energy detectives of all kinds and anyone interested in what used to be called "psychosomatic medicine."

Ill-informed, useless and eccentric literature in this field does exist. These are the books I recommend.

Additional material concerns how one Medical Intuitive views his field and his practice:

- Illness as a healing metaphor.

- Willingness to heal is the pre-requisite to heal

- Summary of some very recent protocols and methods for connecting the dots between illnesses and issues.

Chapter Four has some original research on therapeutic metaphors for illness: Cancer and tumors in general, Stroke, SIDS, Autism, Alzheimer's, ADHD, Attention deficit, Hyperactive disorder.

A Proposed Wikipedia page upgrade on "Medical Intuitive"

4) *Your Habit Body,* An Owner's Manual

Your Habit Body
An Owner's Manual
A three selves journal

Bruce Dickson
HealingCoach.org

Our Habit Body is our best and closest friend. It remembers every routine thing we do daily--so we don't have to relearn all our habits all over again each day. Habits are reactivity set on automatic, behavior conditioned to repeat.

If this is so, how come the one thing human beings do better than anything else is to make the same mistake over and over and over again?

Based on results, we don't know as much about our habit body as people think. We need new Tools That Heal to get at the 90% of our habit body that is sub- and unconscious.

We have habits on five personality levels: physical, imaginal, emotional, mental and unconscious. How are they organized? How do we keep all our habits organized so when we wake up in the morning, we don't have to relearn everything? Personal-spiritual growth is upgrading our habits on any of these levels.

Sound like a lot to manage? This makes your job easier, the missing manual for anyone who owns a Habit Body.

We used to say, "He who doesn't know his history is doomed to repeat it." We can say more precisely, "Whoever neglects their habit body will have the same behaviors and results tomorrow, as they did yesterday." Find answers here:

- Why we were more lovable when we were young

- Every day we are "training a new puppy"

- Why 90% of habits are invisible in 3D

- A dozen common terms for the "habit body."

Garrison Keillor says, "Culture is what you know is so by age 12." ALL culture can be seen as just a bunch of habits, including your own. Once you can see it, you can redirect it. 78 pages.

5) You are a Hologram Becoming Visible to Your Self

You are a Hologram
Becoming visible to your self

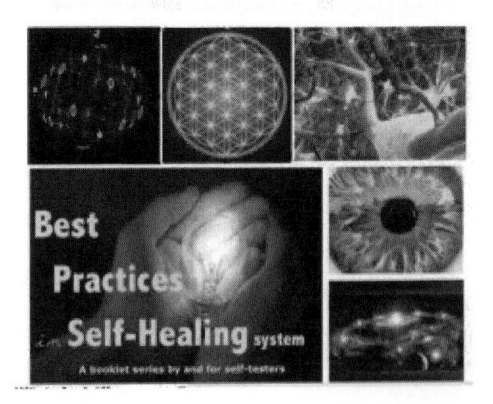

The bigger part of us, our inner child, immune system, high self, "true self," "divine connection"--however you term it, is invisible to us for several reasons--but you can change this and get to know the "bigger you."

The metaphor of a hologram is a good way to see the "bigger you" behind all the familiar smokescreens.

A hologram metaphor assists us to reframe the "bigger you" with new eyes. As modern people, we understand a hologram has both three dimensions and internal structure. These are useful metaphors for our inner dimensions and the structures in our sub- and unconscious. Our psyche is a hologram of physical, imaginal, emotional, mental and mythological potentials. Some are fully activated, many are not. Some are stuck and dysfunctional.

What we have inside us can be understood in terms of a 3D framework and a hologram is the way to "see" this, the structure of the "bigger you."

HealingToolbox.org

A full discussion of how the "bigger you" is structured and organized as a hologram, and the history of this idea, in included in this work.

6) **Self-Healing 101, 2nd Ed.** Seven Experiments in Self-healing You Can Do at Home to Awaken the Inner Healer

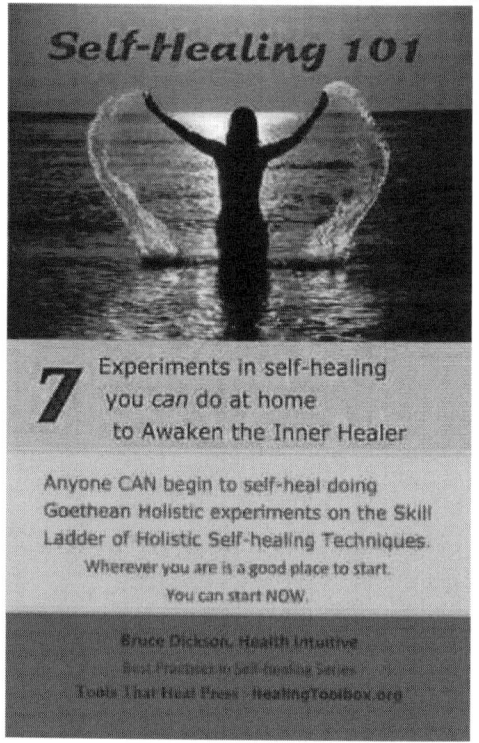

Anyone CAN self-heal. Wherever you are is a good place to start. You can start NOW

For those looking to go deeper into self-healing and/or begin or deepen their practice of self-muscle-testing. Alternatively, for those teaching others how to self-muscle-test.

Self-healing and self-muscle-testing is outside the exhausted residue of Cartesian-Newtonian Science. Self-healing and self-muscle-testing is really part of the more appropriate newer Goethean Holistic Science; that is, all results, all phenomena, are replicable but NOT by all persons, at all places and all times, regardless of intention. Rather results are replicable primarily in the domain of one person.

Q: How do I begin our own journey of self-healing in the domain of one person, myself?

A: We move to a more experiential approach to self-healing beginning with

- Self-acceptance, self-love

- prayers of self-protection

- self-sensitivity

- self-permission to make testing experiments.

In hands-on Goethean Holistic Science experiments, there is no penalty for failure, none at all--as long--as you learn something from every experiment.

The only wrong way to experiment is not to try at all.

7) "Willingness to heal is the pre-requisite for all healing"

Willingness to Heal ~ 111

"Willingness to heal is the prerequisite for all healing"

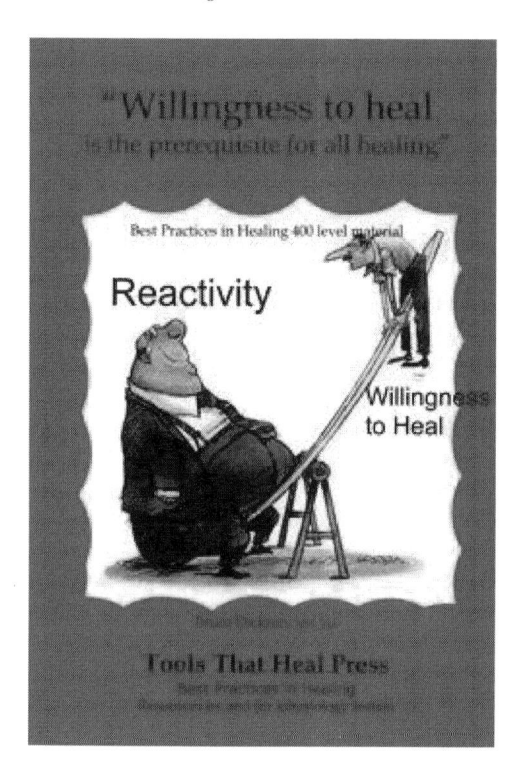

Best Practices in Healing 400 level material

Reactivity

Willingness to Heal

Tools That Heal Press

This quote from Bertrand Babinet begins exploration and expansion of some of Bertrand Babinet's wonderful legacy of theory and method.

If you can do kinesiology testing by any method, you can measure your own willingness to heal. Self-testers can measure their own willingness to heal, in your inner child.

This tells you if your silent partner is ready to heal what you wish to heal. You can use this to explore where you are most ready to grow.

Have clients? The effectiveness of any energetic session can be estimated AHEAD OF TIME, with surprising accuracy--before you begin working! Practitioners in any and all modalities, are encouraged measure willingness to heal FIRST!

HealingToolbox.org

Save your self from wasting effort when clients are of two minds on their issue and do not know this. The higher the number on a scale of 1-10, the more momentum your client has to heal on that issue.

Willingness to heal is the key to aligning and integrating the three selves. Willingness is where the whole topic of the 3S leads.

NOTE ~ This booklet assumes readers can already either self-test using kinesiology testing—K-testing, dowsing, or some other form; or, can follow instructions to use any partner to do two-person testing, termed Client

Controlled Testing. Problems with your own testing? Don't trust your own results? See the training protocol breakthroughs in Self-Healing 101.

8) *You Have Three Selves;* Simplest, clearest model of the Whole Person, Volume ONE, Orientation

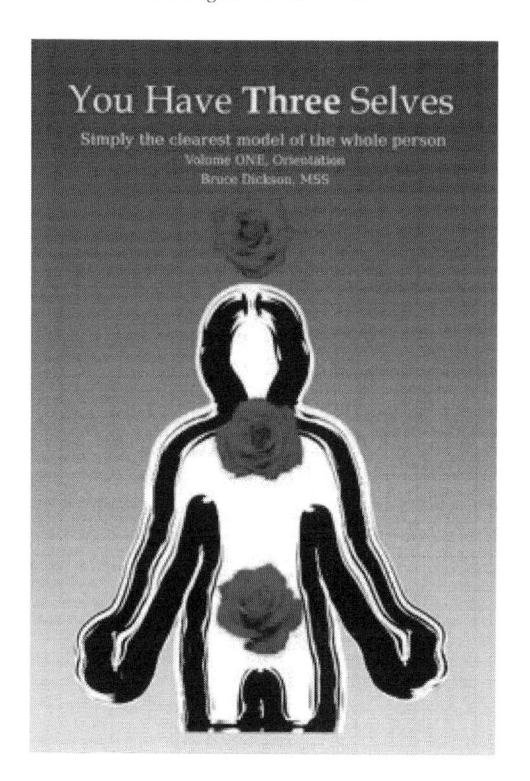

Compose your own vision of self-healing with the first comprehensive general textbook on the Three Selves. The basic self is functionally equal to the inner child, Little Artist, immune system and 12 other 20th century terms. The conscious self is your rational mind, which can be either feeling or thinking! Your high self is your guardian angel, your own higher Guidance. Aligning all three of these on the same goal so they can work as a team, describes much of what we do in 3D embodiment. Written with diagrams and much humor. 223 p. 6x9"

9) *You Have Three Selves;* Simplest, clearest model of the Whole Person; Volume TWO, Finding the 3S in Your Life

If the Three Selves are universal and pervasive in psychology, they ought to be visible all around us. Yikes, it's true! Find the 3S in your body, in pop culture, in the fun of Transactional Analysis, etc. 93 p. 6x9"

Unconscious Patterns 101, *Tools for the Hero's Journey of Self-healing*

Picking up where NLP metaprograms left off, expanding the topic in the context of 'God is my Partner.'

Unconscious Patterns 101
Tools for the Hero's Journey of Self-healing

Identify, address and clear
with 'God as my Partner'

Tools That Heal Press

How does our UNconscious work? It works according to PATTERNS. FRACTAL patterns also play a part.

Invisible patterns in our psyche is relatively new so this is a basic intro. NLP's Metaprograms are a crucial part of this. The Appendix contains a summary of NLP metaprograms. Games People Play and Scripts People Live, as well. TA's coverage of these role-playing games is so good, no need to repeat them here.

Unconscious patterns live in our habit body, our nearest and closest partner and teammate, carrying all the sub- and unconscious patterns we use to get thru each day.

The more aware we are of unconscious patterns, the more able we are to address and tweak dysfunctions.

HealingToolbox.org

Our job as conscious-waking self, is to remain "at choice" because 'Soul is choice.' Only since 1990 have we had any reliable experimental method to explore, navigate and remediate invisible unconscious patterns: Muscle testing, 20 or more methods, is the modern way to make changes and upgrade Unconscious patterns we wish to change.

10) Muscle Testing as a Spiritual Exercise; Building a Bridge to Your Body's Wisdom

Muscle Testing as a Spiritual Exercise
Building a Bridge to Your Body's Wisdom

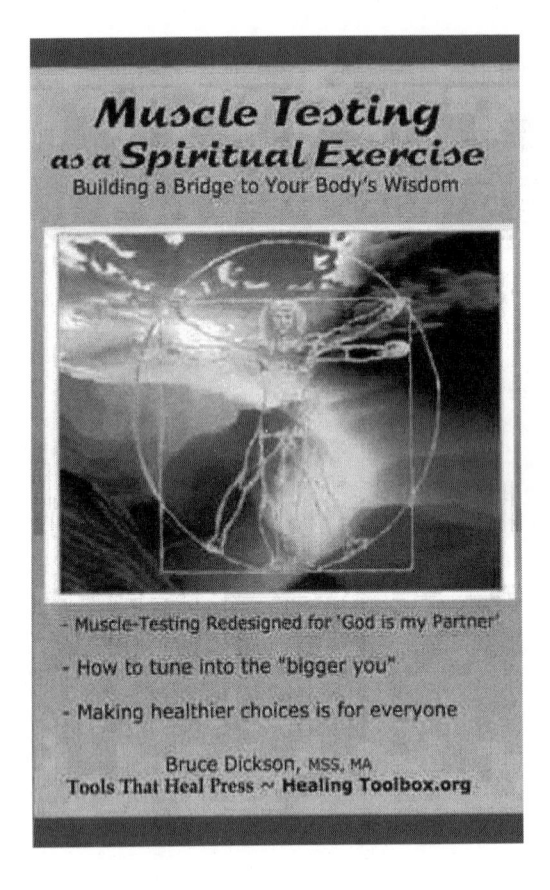

- Muscle-Testing Redesigned for 'God is my Partner'
- How to tune into the "bigger you"
- Making healthier choices is for everyone

Bruce Dickson, MSS, MA
Tools That Heal Press ~ Healing Toolbox.org

- Muscle-Testing Redesigned for 'God is my Partner'

- How to tune into the "bigger you"

- Making healthier choices is for everyone

The Healing Toolbox approach to "how to do muscle testing."

To write this, almost the whole modern history of muscle testing had to be stood on its head. Everything I had learned from dowsing and Touch for Health, conventional muscle testing, had to be DIS-connected from Cartesian-Newtonian science; then, re-contexted inside Goethean Holistic Science. Consequently, this is NOT your mother's-father's kinesiology manual.

22 videos are also referenced and their topics are expanded on here.

Our small intestine is already muscle testing 24/7. As waking-conscious selves, we can re-arrange our thinking to use this to our advantage. It requires some lively conceptual ju-jitsu. I believe the journey will be both practical and entertaining.

ANY method on the Skill Ladder of Holistic Self-healing Techniques-Methods-Arts is useful on a Heroes Journey of Self-healing. Cessation of inner againstness and releasing of outworn "stories" PACME is always good.

The Skill Ladder is here: "A clear skill ladder exists of holistic self-healing methods-techniques-arts"
http://www.healingtoolbox.org/k2-stub/item/333-skill-ladder-of-holistic-healing-methods-techniques-arts

This book address primarily only the technique-method-art of self-muscle-testing.

Arm-length-testing is preferred for beginners over all

other methods. Any other method of muscle testing is fine too. Arm-length-testing is here: http://innerwise.com/en/videos/all-videos/113-innerwise-the-arm-lenght-test?category_id=54

Same book simultaneously published under three different tiles-covers but same insides

Muscle Testing for Success; Muscle-testing exercises applied to success topics.

Simultaneously published as *Success Kinesiology, Dowsing for Success* and *Muscle Testing for Success*. All editions virtually the same except for unique covers.

12) COMING 2015

Measuring, math and scales--with 'God as my Partner

Measuring
with 'God as your Partner'
Scales of 2, 5, 10, 100 and 1000

Make a pie chart graph of any health concern
Algebra for addressing unknown disturbances
Letting the inner Traveler pick the issues you work on today

This way

him   **That way**

now   her

X   then

Y

Best Practices in Self-Healing System
A booklet series by and for self-testers & Healing Buddies

Many Goethean Science experiments in self-testing to explore, experiment and expand skills in self-healing. Written for dowsers, self-testers, self-healers and those wishing to improve their self-testing.

ALL exercises here REQUIRE familiarity and/or some skill with muscle testing, kinesiology testing, dowsing.

If you like and dislike things, you are already measuring invisible--still real things. Every time you choose one option over another, you are measuring invisibles.

You measure if the weather is too hot or too cold to wear this or that clothing. If you sing, you are constantly measuring to stay on key. If you dance, you are constantly measuring if your are following the rhythm or not. All these things are invisible.

May as well get good at measuring invisibles, we do it every day.

When we add scales and numbers to our unconscious measuring exercises, we include, train and strengthen the conscious-waking self.

With children, after age seven, to support their conscious self, we encourage accurate counting of physical items via math manipulatives.

For adults, counting invisible things precisely is mostly called "muscle testing," sometimes "dowsing." Muscle testing of any kind strengthens the conscious self even more quickly than math manipulatives because we are attending to real things that while unseen, are still countable.

The healthy human being is the primary and sometimes only accurate measuring tool for measuring character, as we do in voting, elections and mate selection. May as well get good at it!

13) *The Inner Court: Close-up of the Habit Body*

The Inner Court
Close-up of the habit body
How Guinevere, Lancelot, Merlin & Arthur influence you every day

Bruce Dickson, MSS

Building on Your Habit Body, An Owner's Manual, our gut brain (inner child) is shown to have four quadrants. This is the next logical level deeper than the inner child, the beginning of the Fractal Personality.

The four archetypal characters of Camelot, Guinevere, Lancelot, Merlin & King Arthur (GLMA) have long-served as lenses for insight into our own subconscious role playing. Add muscle testing, and you can use them to navigate your habit body to what is working and not working in your psyche. It becomes possible to see where our habits, behaviors, and comfort zones are running, repeating and where we can make changes.

Functional~dysfunctional expressions of each member of the Inner Court are provided. This erects a body-centric map to locate where everyday disturbances originate and track back to. If you can feel it—and locate it--you can heal it!

All aspects of the Inner Court lends itself highly to muscle testing experiments.

The Inner Court is a "magic mirror," reflecting our preferred memories, habits and behaviors in body image, posture, attire, accessories and so on.

These four are the KEY ACTORS in our habit body, acting out preferences, memories, habits and behaviors. They are the "script writers," script holders, and role-playing actors, "holding court" in our sub- and unconscious. They determine our habitual memories, habits, behaviors, routines and preferences.

Q: What's left for ME to do?

A: YOU remain Director of this UNconscious "writers room" and acting company.

Soul is choice; nothing determines our personality—unless we allow it. However, we rely on the acquired habits of our Inner Court to suggest how to respond to life situations. If we do not change how we respond, we WILL respond in the habitual ways our Inner Court knows to respond.

Say you are feeling bad. You can ask, Who inside me feels unresolved? Oh, it's Guinevere! She feels rejected. Let's see why she feels that way and what she needs."

The health and strength of each quadrant is easily assessed and measured with kinesiology testing, muscle testing, of any kind.

These insights have been extensively tested by the author in client sessions since 2001. Insights gleaned from the Inner Court easily transfer to working with clients.

Bertrand Babinet's original names for each quadrant was, Mother, Child, Grandparent, Father.

Readers familiar with Virginia Satir's Stress Response Stances will see the connection and one of the likely origins here.

The Inner Court IS the inner child, in a four-fold, close-up view. It's a more exact, body-based, imagining of "inner child, four times more precise. This map of inner child is four times as precise as Bradshaw's unitary concept of the "inner child."

Arthurian legend always had, always was, a map, a guide, to possible behaviors and expressions possible in the human experience, both functional and dysfunctional.

The map does not determine the territory; the Inner Court does not determine personality. Yet, our every possible like & dislike, strength & weakness, are all "programmed" into the firmware of our habit body. The Inner Court is how to view them so you can learn from and initiate change as you see fit. If you can access a dysfunctional habit, there is Grace available to redirect, upgrade, change or release it.

The purpose of the Inner Family in the gut is highly involved with developing healthy self-esteem from conception to age 11. Before puberty, the locus of control in our psyche is our gut brain in theta. After puberty, locus of control shifts from gut to head brain-spine. The relative activity and interaction of self-esteem and self-concept, presages personality.

Further into our Fractal Psyche, we have TWO Inner Courts, one in our gut brain, a second one in the four brain quadrants. Our cerebral cortex, also has four discernible quadrants but in different order and in a plane turned 90 degrees from the gut brain.

The archetypes of Arthurian legend in the head are highly tied with developing self-concept.

The two Courts make the previously mysterious topics of self-esteem and self-concept understandable.

Q: What is the goal of a quadrant?

A: The goal for each is acknowledgement, safety, trust, connection, cooperation, mutual support and teamwork with the other three in its system. The strength and weakness of relationships between any two members is easy to measure. In this, the Inner Court is the beginning of the Inner Dashboard, the safe and appropriate place for us to work to make changes in our own psyche.

In the six possible relationships between the four archetypes, our personal failures, confusions and successes are expressed and can be easily diagrammed towards understanding our behavior.

The Inner Court makes obvious the strengths and weaknesses of many previous mysteries:

- The limitations of "right and left brain" are completed here in a quadrant system,

- Personality typology in general is clarified,

- The connection between neurotransmitter production and the Inner Court becomes clear,

- The classic Supporter, Promoter, Analyzer, Controller typologies,

- MBTI ideas of how personality is formed thru preferences,

- Aristotle's & Rudolf Steiner's four Temperaments,

- The pioneering work of Ned Herrmann & Katherine Benziger is clarified and made more artistic.

The Inner Court model is appropriate to grad students and ANYONE interested in counseling, coaching, training, sales and personal growth. 116 p. 6x9"

14) The Five Puberties, a Three Selves Journal on Children

You Have Five Puberties
A Three Selves journal on Children
The Three Selves in stage-development terms

Bruce Dickson, MSS, MA

Growing new eyes to see children and stage-development afresh is the goal of this booklet. It builds on the foundation of the other volumes—or--can be read alone. Children are viewed thru lenses not often used: body posture, stories the body tells, animals, plants, the succession of puberties--at least four puberties--each of us undergoes on our journey towards independent thinking.

Finally, we glance at what progress has been made towards a functional typology of children's temperaments in Anthroposophy, MBTI and Katherine Benziger, providing some directions for fruitful further study. The perplexing problem of how children's typology differs from adult typology, is brought close to resolution.

15) Radical Cellular Wellness—Especially for Women

**Radical Cell Wellness--
Especially for *Women!***

Why cells get sick and how to help them
Cell psychology for everyone
Cellular awakening explained

Health Intuitive Bruce Dickson

Tools That Heal Press
Tools by and for self-healers and self-muscle-testers.
Composing your own vision of self-healing
Best Practices in Healing System ~ 400 level material

Cell psychology for everyone; a coherent theory of illness and wellness.

Finally a Theory of Illness and a Theory of How We Heal for everyone—especially for women: your cells are born healthy; and left on their own, cells remain healthy and reproduce perfectly. It is only environmental and human pollution that interferes with cell health and reproduction.

The various forms of internal pollution we allow, promote and create are discussed with an eye to solutions!

Works incidental & complementary to Best Practices Series, above

- *Rudolf Steiner's Fifth Gospel in Story Form*

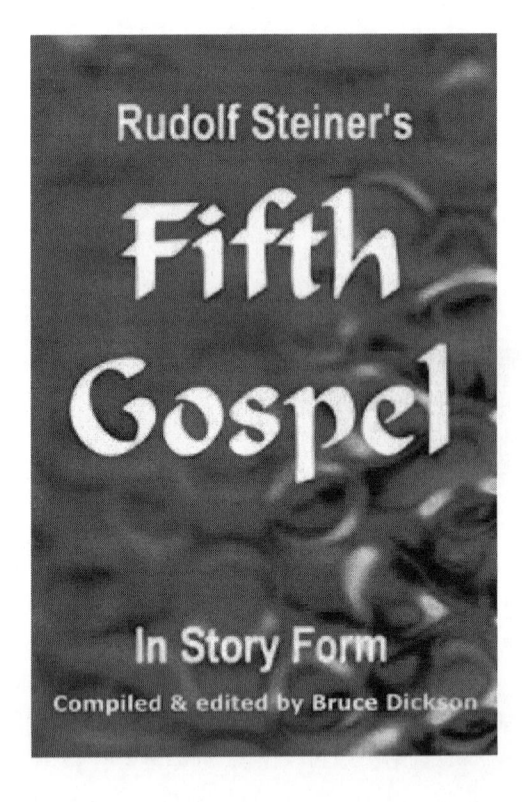

One of the wonderful experiences of my Waldorf teacher training was in a comfy living room, with a group of friends, reading aloud Rudolf Steiner's Fifth Gospel transcripts, round-robin style, a paragraph at a time. We read a chapter each night over the 12 Days of Christmas. If you've done this, maybe you also felt the pull to draw closer to this material. I certainly did.

Dr. Steiner's aim was to update the biography of Jesus of Nazareth, in light of the expanded psychological understanding of karma and reincarnation flourishing in the West between 1880 and 1920.

HealingToolbox.org

The imaginative capacity of humankind, our increased ability to process metaphor, demonstrated by Depth Psychology and Carl Jung, made possible this portrait of Jesus of Nazareth and what he transformed into. RS's Fifth Gospel remains the most psychologically astute portrait of Jesus of Nazareth this author is aware of.

An unexpected function of this material is it can support people who have lost the thread of connection with their own internal Christ spark, our immortal-eternal soul. Steiner's Fifth Gospel is an opportunity to pick up the thread of their own connection again. RS's ideas can be very healing to many conventional ideas about Jesus of Nazareth.

What Steiner found in the Akashic Records, regarding the life of Jesus of Nazareth, was a series of "story book images." These are apparently quite closely and faithfully approximated by both children's Sunday School images of the life of Christ; and also by, traditional stained glass windows of the Stations of the Cross.

If you know him, you won't be surprised to hear Steiner dove into and behind these images to penetrate their inner reality; and then, articulate it in modern language for modern minds.

Steiner's verbatim lecture transcripts of his investigations were published in a book called The Fifth Gospel, but his basic clairvoyant research was never compiled nor edited; nor, was any attention paid to building a mood.

Topics include:

Inner experience of the disciples at Pentecost.

The two Jesus children, tradition of and evidence for.

Contribution of the Buddha to the Luke Jesus child.

The shepherds see the astral body of Buddha.

- *How We Heal; and, Why do we get sick?*

How We Heal
And, Why do we get sick?
And 35 better, more precise questions,
answered by a Medical Intuitive
Bruce Dickson, MSS, MA

If I'm middle-aged or older, is it too late to change?
Why does God allow physical pain?
How come I know so little about healing myself?
Can you help me see disease from Spirit's point of view?
Where is a coherent theory of illness and wellness?
What do I have to know to heal my self?
What are trapped emotions? How do I release them?
Why won't God help me with my dis
How do I get the attention of a Benefact
Is this a disturbance or a clearing
How much of my disease is geneti
What can illness teach us? What can I learn from
Where does disease come from?
Is examining past lives foolish escapism?
How come   bad things in past lives?
Why d   l it, you can heal it"?
What's the e   solved childhood issues?
H   we   ing process?
t sh   I get sick?
n I b   n doctor?
How do I take ba   my power,   ck my health from doctors?
H w do Medica   ntuitives work
What does effective healing loo ke from Spi t's point of view?
What are Best   eal ng?
hat does   it d?
If cells a e cons   iselves,
why ren   t?

Including 35 better, more precise questions on wellness and healing, answered by a Medical Intuitive

HealingToolbox.org

Why every illness is a healing metaphor A theory of Cellular Awakening, short version.

Your personal beliefs & myths about healing.

#1: If we understand our problems, they will be healed.

#2: If you don't know and don't understand, then you can't heal.

#3: Personal-spiritual change takes a long time and is always a slow process. After all, you've had the problem for a long time.

#4: If you've had a negative belief for a long time, it will take a long time to change.

#5: If you change quickly, it must be superficial and not long lasting.

#6: I can't change; "This is the way I am; I'll always be this way."

#7: If you are middle-aged or older, it is too late to change.

#8: Changing old behaviors and thought patterns is often difficult and painful, "No pain, no gain."

Why is pain allowed? Why do I put up with so much pain in my body?

Can you help me see disease from Spirit's point of view?

18 more questions--answered!

Holistic Chamber Start-up Kit (2009 edition)

Everything you need to start your own local Holistic Chamber of Commerce .A fundraiser for local HCCs everywhere!

Each copy purchased benefits the local Chamber you buy it from. Bruce Dickson, Founder, Co-Chair ToolsThatHeal.com ~ HealingCoach.org

Camille Leon, Co-Chair ~ Westside Holistic Chamber of Commerce & http://www.holisticchamberofcommerce.com

8,000 words to inspire you to start a local chamber, where the network is, tips and hard-won experience to save you time on the front end. Concludes with some ideas you can implement once you get going.

Connect with the Author

Find Bruce at http://www.HealingToolbox.org

Gift initial sessions available for a while longer.

Bruce has a series of 15 books, 20 videos and the Inner Dashboard method.

Sessions with the author

Gift initial sessions available for a while longer.

HealingToolbox.org

Between 8:00 am and 9:00 pm PST.

HealingToolbox@gmail.com   Skype: SelfHealingCoach

Health Intuitive Bruce Dickson shows people how to use their own Inner Dashboard so they can increase their own Inner Sunshine. How? By identifying and removing blocks and obstacles to inner Light & Sound.

With your permission, Bruce talks directly with your immune system and your own Guidance, to learn what's oppressing your cells. He shows you how to throw off burdens you no longer wish to carry.

"Working from my own limited mind is inefficient and not much fun. It works better to work from your own higher Guidance. Your Benefactors know you better than I; they know the path to your next healing better than I, so I let them lead."

Want homework? Many ways to connect with your own Guidance exist thru the Skill Ladder of Holistic Self-healing Techniques-Methods-Arts.

Let's all use more Tools That Heal and apply Best Practices in Self-Healing; including, Slow-Motion Forgiveness(SM).

Money-back guarantee on all work.

Training with the Author

If you can't go backwards

and can't remain where you are,

I encourage you to begin your own Heroes journey of self-healing.

If you are a holistic practitioner looking for more Tools That Heal and/or develop your own system, let's talk. Video class in the works.

Between 8:00 am and 9:00 pm PST.

HealingToolbox@gmail.com   Skype: SelfHealingCoach

Other products

Slow-Motion Forgiveness ™ Practice CD

The Five Puberties, a 3S journal on Children, 40 p. 6x9"

The Meaning of Illness Is Now an Open Book, Free 31 page PDF by request.

Muscle Testing Practice Group DVD. One hour.

1:1 phone sessions available. Group classes available. Training to do what I do is available.

Reading Group Guide for Self-healing Series

Best sellers

3) Meridian Metaphors, Psychology of the Meridians

HealingToolbox.org

and Major Organs

11) The NEW Energy Anatomy: Nine new views of human energy; No clairvoyance required.

1) You have FIVE bodies PACME; Spiritual Geography 101. The "map" in use by all Light & Sound groups (99 cents).

2) The Meaning of Illness is Now an Open Book, Reference books to cross-reference illness and issues.

4) Your Habit Body, An Owner's Manual, the lower one-third of the "bigger you."

5) You are a Hologram Becoming Visible to Yourself

6) Self-Healing 101, Nine Experiments in Self-healing, You Can Do at Home to Awaken the Inner Healer

7) "Willingness to heal is the pre-requisite for all healing"

8) You Have Three Selves Vol. ONE; Simply the clearest model of the whole-person; Orientation

9) You Have Three Selves; Vol. TWO, Find the 3S in your life & pop culture

10) Muscle Testing as a Spiritual Exercise;

Building a Bridge to Your Body's Wisdom

12) Muscle Testing with scales of 2, 10, 100 & 1000

Measuring invisible energies with 'God as your Partner'

More advanced titles

13) The Inner Court: Close-up of the Habit Body

14) The Five Puberties, Growing new eyes to see children and maturation afresh.

15) Radical Cell Wellness—Especially for women!

Books outside the Best Practices Series

Rudolf Steiner's Fifth Gospel in Story Form

Stand-alone 99 cent eBooks tangential to Best Practices Series

From Five Animal Senses to 12 or More Human Senses

Forgive from Your Soul, Slow Motion Forgiveness, the Missing Manual

How We Heal; and, Why do we get sick? Including 35 more precise Q&A on wellness.

Other CLASSICS of self-healing & Medical Intuition

MSIA Discourses http://www.msia.org/discourses

HealingToolbox.org

www.msia.org

Forgiveness, Key to the Kingdom, John-Roger

The Emotion Code, Bradley Nelson

Messages From the Body, Michael Lincoln

Our Many Selves, Elizabeth O'Connor

Touch for Health, 2nd Ed, Mathew Thie

Your Body Speaks Your Mind, 2nd ed. Deb Shapiro

Core Transformation, Connierae Andreas

The best solution is always loving

Did you enjoy this? Please share.

If you get stuck, give me a call.

What if a fraction of the new replacement culture, you and I are creating now, will begin around self-healing and training activity as the cultural benefit of the hard work of building new, sustainable, intentional community?

Printed in Great Britain
by Amazon.co.uk, Ltd.,
Marston Gate.